TATIANA PROSKOURIAKOFF

TATIANA PROSKOURIAKOFF
Interpreting the Ancient Maya

BY CHAR SOLOMON

UNIVERSITY OF OKLAHOMA PRESS • NORMAN

This book is published with the generous assistance of The Kerr Foundation, Inc.

Page ii: Detail from The Red House at Chichén Itzá, by Tania, at the Peabody Museum, Harvard University. Courtesy of President & Fellows of Harvard College, Peabody Museum, Harvard University (N28438). *Page iii*: Tania, undated. Courtesy of Mike Beetem.

Library of Congress Cataloging-in-Publication Data

Solomon, Char, 1949–
    Tatiana Proskouriakoff : interpreting the ancient Maya / Char Solomon.
        p.   cm.
    Includes bibliographical references and index.
    ISBN 0–8061–3445–3 (hc : alk. paper)
    1. Proskouriakoff, Tatiana, 1909–   2. Mayan languages—Writing.   3. Inscriptions, Mayan.   4. Names, Mayan.   5. Women archaeologists—Latin America—Biography.   6. Women epigraphists—Latin America—Biography.   I. Title.

F1435.3.W75 P767 2002
980.03'092—dc21
[B]

                                                    2002020561

The paper in this book meets the guidelines for permanence and durability of the committee on Production Guidelines for Book Longevity of the Council on Library Resources, Inc. ∞

1 2 3 4 5 6 7 8 9 10

To Tom, who helped me believe, and

to Sean and Kate, that they may know no limits.

CONTENTS

CONTENTS

ILLUSTRATIONS

PREFACE

Most of the people I have viewed as heroes in my life have been women. First it was my grandmother; later, Amelia Earhart, Jane Goodall, and Joann Andrews. They inspired me with their strength, purpose, and commitment to excellence. There have been men too, but I believe there is a great need for more women role models, positive women making definite contributions in their lifetimes. Tatiana Proskouriakoff, who left her mark on Maya archaeology at a time when the field was still dominated by gentlemen explorers and scholars, is one such woman.

I had the privilege of working for Tania, as her friends and colleagues called her. In 1972 I walked into the Peabody Museum of Archaeology and Ethnology at Harvard University with the hope of finding work. The woman behind the desk said that there were no openings, but there might be an opportunity to volunteer. She told me that Tania Proskouriakoff needed an assistant for her catalog of Maya jades, and I caught my breath. The name was familiar to me from college courses in anthropology and art history, and I excitedly agreed to meet with her.

The woman led me through exhibits of Indian artifacts, beadwork, moccasins, and leather clothing. Pushing open a side door, we came to a drab stairwell. Down a flight of steps, we reached the basement and wound our way through a narrow, dark corridor, lined with filing cabinets and labeled drawers. Finally, we stopped at a large, bright room with windows at ground level. Sunlight streamed onto two drafting tables, and classical music came softly from a radio in one corner. A tanned, smiling man turned from one of the tables and said hello in a resonant English accent. In the center of the room, an older woman in dark-rimmed glasses sat working intently at her desk. When she looked up, the woman from the front office introduced us, saying, "Ms. Proskouriakoff, here is someone who may be able to help you with your jade project."

Tania smiled, stood to shake hands, and steered me off to one side of the room. She was a petite woman, in her sixties, with short, tightly curled brown hair. She quietly asked a few questions about my background, looking steadily at me with sharp brown eyes. She spoke quickly, with no discernible accent. I told her that in the past year I had cataloged and mounted an exhibit of Japanese scrolls and another of Hindu sculpture for the college I had attended. This seemed to please her, and she began showing me the small, beautifully carved pieces of jade on her desktop. She explained that they had been dredged from the Sacred Cenote at Chichén Itzá early in the century and that before presenting much of the collection to officials in a ceremony in Mexico City, she was repairing and cataloging them. It was an exacting, time-consuming job, and she wanted to know when I could start and how much time I could devote to the project each week.

In the coming months, as we worked in her office, Tania shared many stories of her childhood and of her early adventures in the remote jungles of Central America, and I listened eagerly to every word. These stories stayed with me over the years and are now a part of this book. Since that time I have worked as a teacher and writer, and as a wife and mother of two wonderful young people I have found inspiration in the lives of strong and compassionate women. Tania is among them.

As I began my work on Tania's biography, I realized this would be a personal journey. It would demand careful research, self-discipline, and honesty. My goal has been to portray Tania's emotional and intellectual growth and the choices and sacrifices she made along the way to becoming one of the foremost Mayanists of the twentieth century. While I have tried to place her in the context of the many colorful and important personalities in the field of Mesoamerican archaeology, a meticulous analysis of her life's work is not within the scope of this book. Such an analysis is important for scholars of the Maya and can be found in technical journals and in such works as the recently published *Decipherment of Ancient Maya Writing*. It is my hope, rather, that this biography will describe the complex life of Tatiana Proskouriakoff and in so doing, help to bring to light the truly exceptional woman she was.

ACKNOWLEDGMENTS

Over these past years, I have had contact with many wonderful people who have made writing this biography a stimulating and rewarding experience. I will always be grateful for their support and many kindnesses. I must give special thanks to Clemency Coggins and Ian Graham, who encouraged me in the early stages to undertake this project. My husband, Tom Oakley, was the first to help me see that I should write Tania's life story and since then has kept me on track with his good humor, guiding hand, and the latest tools for writing and communication. Our two grown children, Sean and Kate, have kept me grounded through it all. Clemency Coggins, Joyce Marcus, Kornelia Kurbjuhn, John Longyear, George Stuart, Ian Graham, Andrew Chenzoff, Tinky Beaver, and my husband have read sections of the manuscript and made timely suggestions as the work progressed. John Longyear and Mark and Jessica Child kindly gave me access to their videotapes of Copán and Piedras Negras, and Ian Graham helped in the selection of appropriate illustrations. On numerous occasions Clemency Coggins extended her warm hospitality to me and my family, as did Kornelia Kurbjuhn and Monni Adams.

Tania's family too has been most supportive. Having access to their photographs, documents, and personal recollections made my research more fruitful. Tania's niece, Norma Jean Ragsdale, warmly provided intimate childhood memories and was always there with encouraging words. Mike Beetem, Tania's nephew, shared his boxes of valuable Proskouriakoff papers and photographs. Tania's cousin, Andrew Chenzoff, provided information and suggestions that were particularly helpful in the early chapters. Other family members to whom I am grateful are Sergei Nekrassoff, Katie and Bonnie Rorrer, and Kathryn Beetem.

I have had the opportunity to meet and to interview many of Tania's friends and colleagues. Their perspectives have been invaluable in producing this book. They include my readers listed above, as well as Ed Shook, Ann Chowning, Gordon Willey, Christopher Jones, Jeremy Sabloff, Peter Mathews, David Kelley, Richard Townsend, William Haviland, Michael Coe, Phillippa Shaplin, Evon and Nan Vogt, Linnea Wren, Monni Adams, Sean Eirik Simpson, David Stuart, Robert McCormick, David Freidel, Henning Siverts, Elizabeth Benson, Richard Woodbury, Susanna Ekholm, Victoria Bricker, Mary Ricketson Bullard, Donald E. Thompson, Stephen Williams, Jerry Epstein, Anne Chapman, and Margaret Harrison.

There are many others who have assisted me in various ways. Olaf Husby provided key information from his research on Gustav Strömsvik, and Anastasia Korolova translated Russian documents from the Proskouriakoff family papers. Ledyard and Jaci Smith and their sister, Camilla, offered insight into the life and career of A. Ledyard Smith. After Ed Shook's death, John Shook made the correspondence between his father and Tania available to me and has been supportive of this project in many ways. Linton Satterthwaite Thorn and Alice Laquer were most helpful with their family history. Matt Schultz gave freely of his information on the Proskouriakoff years in the Philadelphia area, as did Kitty Brumfield, Catherine Hunt, and Holly Reid. Khristaan Villela, Héctor Escobedo, Douglas Givens, Peter Lehnert, Marsh McCall, Harry Pollock, Francie King, Magdalena Ankrum, and Bill Solomon each contributed in some special way to this project.

There were many archivists and librarians without whose assistance this book could not have been written. Outstanding among them are Alex Pezzatti, University of Pennsylvania Museum Archives; John Weeks, Museum Library at the University of Pennsylvania; Sarah Demb, Peabody Museum; Gregory Finnegan, Tozzer Library at Harvard University; Larry Hull, Cannon Memorial Library; Beth Carroll-Horrocks and Rob Cox, American Philosophical Society Library; and Ellen Carpenter and John Strom, Carnegie Institution of Washington Library. Late in this project, Cynthia Close of Documentary Educational Resources was also helpful.

I began work on this book with the aid of a Community Artist Project Grant from the Cabarrus Arts Council. Later I received a North Carolina

Regional Artist Project Grant from the Arts & Science Council–Charlotte/Mecklenburg. This project is made possible in part by a grant from the North Carolina Arts Council, a state agency, the Arts & Science Council-Charlotte/Mecklenburg, Inc., and the arts councils of Anson, Cabarrus, Cleveland, Gaston, Iredell, Lincoln, Rowan, Rutherford, Stanley, Union, and York counties. Their financial support came at a most opportune time.

I would like to thank John Drayton, Jo Ann Reece, and Shelia Buckley of the University of Oklahoma Press. Each helped to keep this project moving forward and was always there with advice and guidance. Finally, I thank my editor, Sheila Berg, who helped to sharpen my text and catch my errors. I have appreciated her patience and careful attention to detail.

TATIANA PROSKOURIAKOFF

CHAPTER ONE

The Russian Years

In winter 1939, just three weeks after her thirtieth birthday, Tania stood alone on the deck of the SS *San Gil*, a banana cargo boat operated by the United Fruit Company. As the boat pulled away from the dock into the Philadelphia harbor, Tania pulled her coat tight and waved to the small group of family and friends who had gathered to see her off. Linton and Peggy Satterthwaite had brought her boxes of candy and cigarettes, and J. Alden Mason, whom she affectionately called Jefe, had given her a bouquet of flowers. Tania's father had said his good-bye earlier that morning as he dashed off to work, and she missed his smiling face among the others on the dock. Her mother, a physician trained in Russia, had given her a box containing vitamins and medicines for the Tropics.[1] Although Tania had traveled to Central America on two previous occasions, this was her first journey alone. It would not be her last. With the loving support of a family deeply committed to excellence, she had been encouraged to develop her talents and pursue her interests even when this led her far from home, to remote archaeological sites in Mexico, Guatemala, and Honduras.

Tatiana Avenirovna Proskouriakoff, "Duchess" to her family and "Tania" to her friends, was born in Siberia on January 23, 1909, the daughter of Alla Nekrassova and Avenir Proskouriakoff. The upheavals affecting the world during the next decade had a dramatic effect on Tania's close-knit family. They helped to shape the brilliant mind that would one day transform the world's view of a vital civilization, the Maya of Central America. To understand the complex and remarkable woman that Tania became, we must look first at her family and the intellectual environment in which she was raised.

Tania's mother was the headstrong daughter of Alexei Nekrassoff, a general in Czar Nicholas's Imperial Army.[2] She was born in Tula on October 1, 1887, and later attended the conservatory in Moscow. In addition to the normal school curriculum, it was customary for the children of families in the upper levels of Russian society to receive training in French, music, and art. Alla became an accomplished pianist and especially loved the compositions of Chopin.

Moscow was a vibrant city at this time, with a booming economy and a rich cultural life. Wealthy families competed to own the finest collection of paintings by French impressionists such as Cézanne and Gauguin, and they regularly attended performances of the Bolshoi Ballet. There were several resident opera company's productions from which to choose during the customary nine-month season, as well as regular performances of plays at the Arts Theatre under the direction of the renowned Konstantin Stanislavsky. This was the city of Alla's childhood before the general strikes of 1905, before the devastation of the Great War and the Russian Revolution.[3]

One summer Alla traveled with her father to southern Siberia, where he was overseeing munitions production for the Imperial Army. On this trip she met a man who captivated her with his intelligence, good looks, and charm. At home with her family, she could not put the man out of her thoughts. Avenir Proskouriakoff, born on July 10, 1884, was the eldest of seven children. His parents, Alexandra and Pavel Stepanovich Proskouriakoff, had met and married while both were attending university in Saint Petersburg. Pavel later accepted a position as proctor in a school in Krasnoyarsk, Siberia, bringing with him his Polish-born wife and their first child, Avenir. The area had been home to generations of Proskouriakoffs since 1698, when their ancestors were banished from Moscow for their involvement in the Strel'tsy Revolt. They had been among the musketeers who were spared from execution by the Russian Empire's ruler, Peter the Great.[4]

While teaching in Krasnoyarsk, Pavel developed an interest in mining. Searching for gold, he discovered instead the remains of a prehistoric mammoth. He excavated the bones and later helped to establish a museum for their display. The center of the region's mining district was in the nearby city of Tomsk, which also had a technical institute and the area's first university, drawing students from the surrounding area. When Avenir completed high school, he enrolled in classes at the Imperial Institute of Technology and began studying for a degree in chemical engineering. In summer 1906 he met and fell in love with Alla.

Convinced that Alla's parents would never approve of their marriage, Alla and Avenir decided to elope. They secretly devised a way for her to return to Tomsk. One day she left for school as expected but went instead to the train station and purchased a ticket on the Trans-Siberian Railroad. She had dutifully written a note telling her family of her intentions. When her father read the note, he sent two of his soldiers to find her and bring her home. The soldiers intercepted the train, but Alla convinced them instead to escort her the rest of the way to Tomsk. These skills of persuasion and determined persistence in the face of great odds proved invaluable to Alla and her family in the turbulent years ahead.[5]

Tomsk, one of Siberia's oldest cities, was founded in 1604 as a fortress on the high banks at the confluence of the Ob and Tom Rivers. The city was home to the Proskouriakoffs for the next nine years. Water was delivered directly to homes in water carts driven by Chinese men, and residents walked along raised wooden sidewalks. These walkways were particularly helpful in September and October, when the unpaved streets turned to mud during the heavy seasonal rains.[6] Winters were dry and cold, but summers were delightful. The young couple enjoyed picnicking with their family and close circle of friends on the riverbanks or taking walks in the rolling countryside outside of town.

Avenir and Alla Proskouriakoff, 1906, Siberia. Courtesy of Mike Beetem.

In 1907 their first child was born, a daughter they named Ksenia. Avenir continued his studies and received a Doctor of Science degree in 1911. He began teaching classes at the institute as an associate professor. Alla enrolled as a student in the medical department the year that the Imperial Tomsk University opened the doors of its medical school to women.[7] Special tutoring was offered to these women in preparation for their difficult coursework. In the coming years Alla worked hard and completed her training. After three months of examinations, on December 3, 1912, she was granted the title Medical Doctor cum laude. For the next two years, Alla worked as an assistant in the medical school's Department of Ophthalmology. Each summer she also served as the resident physician for a small village outside of Tomsk. The village provided a comfortable dacha as their family home for these months.

Avenir's father, Pavel, had accepted a position at the university teaching natural science. He wrote articles on Siberian archaeology, which were published in the local newspaper. In 1981 Tania related a story about some of his students who had become unhappy about a government decree dissolving political clubs. Only one club, the Academicians, was permitted, because it claimed to avoid politics and to focus only on studies. Believing the club was tolerated because it was pro-czarist, the other students staged a demonstration. When a local paper ran a story on the demonstration, an unidentified group beat the owner of the newspaper. Both student groups claimed the other was responsible, and when they gathered a fight broke out. The police were called in to break up the disturbance and to search the basements of the dormitories for subversive material. Hoping to give the students enough time to get rid of incriminating evidence, Pavel refused the police entry. With special orders, the police entered and found printing presses and student protest pamphlets.[8] Similar to the official response during the Moscow University disturbances of 1910–11, the elder Proskouriakoff was demoted to teaching in the lower school as punishment for his role in the incident.

By 1911 much of Russia was beginning to experience the unrest that ultimately led to the Great Revolution of 1917. Czar Nicholas had suffered a humiliating defeat in an unpopular yearlong war with Japan in 1905 over land claims in the East, and in 1906 he dissolved the first elected Duma, a legislative body with the power to approve or reject laws proposed by the government. The Duma, which intended to distribute state, imperial, and church land to the peasants, survived only seventy-three days.[9]

In the midst of this turmoil, Alla gave birth to her second daughter, Tatiana, whom they called Tania. In 1918, the Bolshevik government converted from the Julian to the Gregorian calendar so that Russian dates would correspond with those of the Western world. Thirteen days were added to the calendar, making Tania's birthdate January 23, 1909. She was one year and nine months younger than her sister Ksenia, who was now affectionately called Cassia by her family.

Like their mother, the two girls were taught French, music, and art. Tania was able to read by the age of three. Late in life she recalled an incident relating to this. As a very young child, while traveling by boat

Grandmother Nekrassova, Ksenia (Cassia), Tatiana (Tania), and Alla Proskouriakoff, Siberia, 1914. Courtesy of Mike Beetem.

to Mongolia with her family, she spotted a camel tied up on deck. She
was naturally curious and wanted to go to look more closely at it. Her
aunt said that camels spit and that Tania ought to sit next to her and read
the newspaper instead. This required self-control for one so young and
spirited.[10]

Avenir and Pavel were both kept busy with their teaching duties, as
education reform had doubled the number of Russian children in schools
by 1912. The goal of the government was to have universal education
by 1922, but world and national events prevented this from becoming
a reality. On June 28, 1914, Archduke Ferdinand of Austria was assas-
sinated in Sarajevo by a Serbian nationalist and in spite of diplomatic
efforts on all sides, by August 1914 Germany and Russia were at war.[11]

By mid-October Warsaw was under attack by German troops and the
Russian army had been devastated at Tannenberg. Alla tensely sought
news of her father, who was commanding his Imperial Army troops, but

word from the front was scarce. The increasingly corrupt Russian cabinet believed the war would not last more than a year and, confident that foreign supplies would be sufficient, decided against building domestic munitions factories. With arms in short supply, there were reports of soldiers being sent into battle without even a bayonet. Avenir could not enlist in the army because of a heart condition[12] brought on by a childhood bout of rheumatic fever, but, with his training in chemistry, he was commissioned to oversee the production of armaments that the United States was selling to Russia. This work in America became crucial to the Russian war effort.

With rapidly deteriorating conditions in their homeland, the family packed their belongings. In late fall 1915 they began the trip north to the White Sea port of Arkhangel'sk to book passage to New York. As the train traveled west through the country beyond Tomsk, it stopped regularly at stations filled with troops. Wounded soldiers, returning from the front, mingled with fresh volunteers leaving their homes in the flood of replacements needed to keep the Germans at bay. Boiling water was available at each stop,[13] and the family carried a treasured samovar, in which they made tea to sustain them on their journey.

The trip was long and difficult, but Avenir was determined to take his family with him to America. In the busy railroad hub of Saint Petersburg, they crowded onto the train headed for Arkhangel'sk, one of only three ports where shipments of arms and ammunition were arriving from the United States and Great Britain. At Arkhangel'sk they hurried through streets piled high with unprotected war supplies awaiting transport to the front. With only a short time remaining before the port would be completely iced in for the season, Avenir secured passage with the Russian East-Asiatic Steamship Company on the *Czaritza* bound on December 2 for New York. They boarded, but it soon became apparent that the ship was already icebound. An icebreaker repeatedly tried to free the ship, but no sooner was the ice broken than it quickly froze again. Both Tania and Cassia were exhausted, sick with measles and scarlet fever. When the captain learned of their illnesses, he ordered them off the ship. Wrapped in blankets, they were carried by soldiers over the ice back to the docks.[14] Alla remained with her daughters, watching as the ship, which had been finally freed from the ice, moved out of the harbor.

It was a difficult decision for Avenir to leave his wife and daughters behind, but he knew the urgency of his work. The transatlantic passage was dangerous and tense. The Germans had heavily mined the waters along the east coast of Scotland, and they had recently increased their use of submarines to control the waters in the North Atlantic.[15] Although Avenir's sense of duty carried him on, he did not know when or if he would see his family and country again.

In Arkhangel'sk, the authorities gave Alla permission to keep her daughters in an empty hospital used in the warmer months for treating cholera patients. Clumps of their hair had begun to fall out, but the girls were able to rest and get the medication they needed. Alla nursed them gently until they were strong enough to travel again. They then traveled by train back to Saint Petersburg where relatives had offered them space in their home.

The weeks dragged on. Alla waited anxiously for news of her husband's arrival, but none came. Finally, on January 10, after depositing more than $2,500 in the National City Bank of New York, Avenir cabled his wife money through the Russo-Asiatique Banque. Later, from his room in the Hotel Belleclaire in New York City at Broadway and 77th Streets, he wrote her a letter.[16] Urging them along on their difficult journey, he tried to soothe the fears Alla had expressed in a letter he kept folded in his wallet. He described the strange and wonderful things he had seen since arriving, the elevated trains and the great variety of people. He sent them a copy of *Uncle Tom's Cabin,* illustrated in dark woodblock prints.[17] Alla and the girls read this together, resting and waiting, impatient for the chance to join him.

CHAPTER TWO

A New Beginning (1916–1925)

With the girls healthy once again, Alla felt they were ready to begin their trip to join her husband in New York. Rather than return to Arkhangel'sk, she decided to take a train to the port city of Bergen, on the west coast of Norway. Here she booked passage with the Norwegian America Line, departing for the United States on February 23 aboard the *Kristiani-afjord*. The passenger register and cruise booklet list Alla and her girls among the first-class passengers, with Saint Petersburg as their place of origin. At sea, meals were announced with a bugle call and were served in the first-class salon, with seating assigned by the chief steward. Children under ten and servants were served separately. Amenities on board included a music room and a library from which books could be borrowed.[1] Many years later Tania recalled this part of their journey. The sea was so rough that as the ship rolled with the waves, furniture slid from one side of their room to the other. It was a frightening experience for a child of seven.[2]

The ship arrived safely in New York Harbor sixteen days after departing from Norway, and Avenir joyfully greeted his family on the dock. As they rode through the city, Tania watched eagerly, expecting to see faces as black as those in the illustrations of *Uncle Tom's Cabin*. She was disappointed to find that many of the people she saw were merely varying shades of brown. The elevated trains her father had written about in his letters were a disappointment too. They did not rise up over the roofs of buildings as she had imagined. The tracks were raised on bridges, and she had seen bridges before.[3]

Soon after their arrival, Avenir took his family and a woman Alla had befriended onboard ship to a restaurant. The woman lit a cigarette while waiting for their food but was quickly told by a waiter that women were not allowed to smoke there. Tania looked around, and seeing that men were smoking without being stopped, she turned to her father and exclaimed, "I thought you told me this was a *free* country." She later told friends it was at this moment that she decided she would one day smoke. On her sixteenth birthday, she asked for a cigarette from her sister, lit it, and dramatically entered the room where guests were gathered for her party, no doubt causing quite a stir.[4] Smoking would remain an ever-present part of her life for the next sixty years.

As a member of the Imperial Russian Artillery Commission, Avenir had been inspecting high explosives at several plants in Pennsylvania since arriving in America. He now received orders from the Russian government to oversee the production of timed fuses made to Russian specifications by the Recording and Computing Machines Company in Dayton, Ohio. Avenir found a large, comfortable house on the outskirts of the city where the family settled for the next year.[5] The climate in Ohio—cold, snowy winters and humid summers—was not much different from what they were used to in Tomsk, but most important, they were together again. Wherever they were sent, they would make a good home.

Alla became active in the women's suffrage movement and regularly attended meetings and rallies. Tania and Cassia worked hard studying English with their parents. It was difficult for the girls. They preferred the familiarity of Russian or French, but the Proskouriakoffs were determined that by the time the girls started school they would be proficient in English. As she did so often in her life, Tania threw herself wholeheartedly into mastering this difficult subject. A cousin of Tania's, Andrew

Chenzoff, recalled that Russian was commonly spoken by the many relatives and White Russian friends who frequented the Proskouriakoff home. Tania, however, always spoke in English.[6]

One childhood story from the family's early time in the United States stands out. It illustrates how Tania was already developing a strong sense of self. Alla had hired a woman to take the place of the favorite nanny the family had to leave behind in Tomsk. For a break in the day, the nanny often took the girls for a walk in a nearby park. On one of these walks, Tania was skipping happily, her loosely tied bonnet bouncing on her head. A woman approached who had heard the nanny speaking French. Confident that the child would not understand, she asked, "Allors, quelle est l'enfant terrible?" Who is this trouble maker? Tania stopped short, curtsied, and responded, "C'est moi, Madame! C'est moi!" It is I, Madame! The embarrassed woman hurried away without another word.[7]

Classes began, and the girls wore bonnets and dresses to school as was customary in Russia. At first they were teased, but because they were bright, happy girls, they soon had a close circle of friends.[8] Though the Proskouriakoffs had not joined a church, Tania was aware that most of her girlfriends went to Sunday school. Being invited to go along one day, she asked her mother for permission. She also asked to take a nickel as she had seen the other girls do. After attending Sunday school with her friend for several weeks, Tania told her mother she did not wish to continue. However, already frugal, she asked if she might still have the nickel to spend on penny candy at the store down the street.[9]

Alla and Avenir read the papers each night, eager for news of the war and events in their homeland. By January 1917 word arrived of massive strikes in Moscow and Saint Petersburg, initiated by Bolshevik revolutionaries and stirred on by terrible food shortages and increasingly heavy war casualties. These strikes were the final blow to the ailing imperial government, and in March Nicholas II abdicated his throne. A provisional government was established under the leadership of the Socialist Alexander Kerensky. The Bolsheviks, in turn, overthrew this government. This was harsh news for the Proskouriakoffs, who fully expected to return to Russia when the war was over.

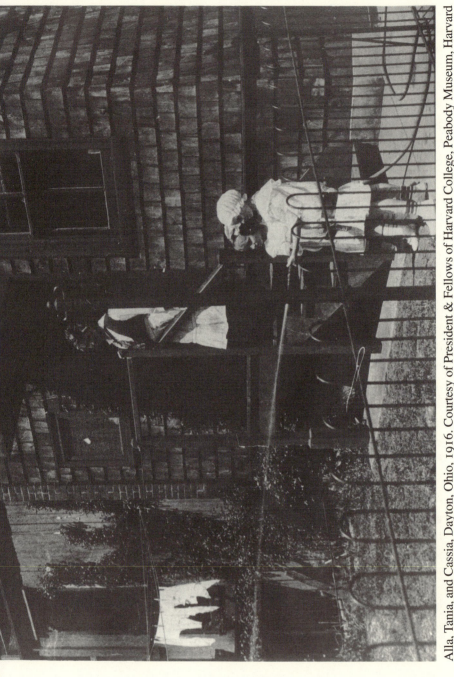

Alla, Tania, and Cassia, Dayton, Ohio, 1916. Courtesy of President & Fellows of Harvard College, Peabody Museum, Harvard University (N 34819).

News of the revolution also affected American companies such as Remington Arms and the Du Pont Corporation, which had been producing munitions under contract with the czarist government. They were suddenly left with costly stockpiles of rifles and ammunition. Another year passed before the U.S. government bought up these munitions and shipped them to Vladivostok on the east coast of Russia to aid the White Russian army's efforts to overthrow the Bolsheviks.[10]

Many displaced Russians found work and settled in and around Philadelphia. This community was made up of a large number of educated professional people, who had fled the strikes, famine, and political upheaval in their country. Many people found jobs in the industrial area along the Delaware River, west of the city. It was in this district that a massive explosion occurred at the Eddystone Ammunition Corporation on the morning of April 10, 1917, just four days after the United States had declared war on Germany. The company was rushing to complete an order for Russia, and workers were loading shells with black explosive powder. An explosion of stockpiled shells suddenly sent shrapnel in all directions and ignited a blaze, killing 139 men and women and wounding many others. German sabotage was initially suspected. After a federal inquiry a decade later, suspicion shifted to Bolshevik sympathizers who were opposed to Russia's involvement in the war.[11] Among the official papers in Avenir's personal files, there is one that, though undated, lists his name as munitions inspector for Eddystone. He may have been one of the inspectors called on to track down the cause of the blast. The document notes that he recommended increased inspection for cracks in all shells.[12] The tragedy touched the Russian community in the Philadelphia area and shocked a nation new to war.

Beginning in 1917, the Proskouriakoffs lived in a number of neighborhoods in the West Philadelphia area. In one of these there were many Jewish families, who impressed Tania for the way the children were encouraged to passionately pursue their interests. Like her family, the parents placed no limits on what their children could aspire to in life. Many years later, while reading a book by Lillian Hellman, Tania came across the name of a boy from one of her old neighborhoods. She remembered that he spent a great deal of time practicing the piano, and through Hellman's book she learned that he had become a successful composer of musical comedy scores. The admiration Tania felt for the Jewish families lasted throughout her life, perhaps in part because it was a Jewish businessman who helped Avenir to get a job as an organic chemist with the chemical company Smith, Klein and French after the czar's abdication left him unemployed.[13]

In 1921 the Proskouriakoffs moved west of Philadelphia to Lansdowne, a lovely borough with tree-lined streets, large homes, and a tradition of excellent schools. In January 1922, Tania completed the eighth grade at the William Cullen Bryant School, and she joined Cassia briefly at West Philadelphia High School. When the family moved into a new home on Fairview Avenue, the girls entered Lansdowne High School, at that time considered one of the best high schools in the state.

Avenir was able to catch the Darby trolley just outside his house at the corner of Fairview and Wycombe Avenues. From Darby, he could go either directly into Philadelphia or to the industrial area in the opposite direction, where his company was located. Alla found work with the school system giving checkups and vaccinations to students. She later was hired by the state and traveled throughout Pennsylvania teaching and supervising midwives.[14]

The family thrived in the friendly environment of Lansdowne. In an interview, Frank Harrison, a retired Lansdowne firefighter who grew up across the street from the Proskouriakoffs, said that they were highly respected in the community. Harrison recalled evenings when Avenir would sit on his front steps with Harrison's father, a biochemist and pharmacologist at the Philadelphia College of Pharmacology and Science. On many summer evenings, the neighborhood children gathered to play ball in the large front yard, and Tania often threw the ball for them.[15] The town's location, midway between the University of Pennsylvania and Swarthmore College, made it a convenient place for many professors to live. Margaret Mead, the noted anthropologist, whom Tania met in later years, lived here while her father taught at the Wharton School of Finance and Commerce at the University of Pennsylvania.[16]

In 1924 the four Proskouriakoffs took the oath of citizenship of the United States, completing their transition to fully committed Americans. As Avenir turned forty, he felt drawn to join a church, and in 1925 he, Alla, and Cassia became members of the Society of Friends in Lansdowne. Tania alone declined.[17] That she was allowed to make this choice for herself at the age of sixteen shows how her parents encouraged independent thinking and action, both of which would be valuable qualities in Tania's years in the field.

Alla and Avenir entertained regularly for their many Russian friends. They drank home-brewed vodka and tea from the samovar. As the evenings progressed, there was singing, dancing, and occasional cursing of the Bolsheviks. At quieter moments Alla played the piano and passed on her love of Chopin to Tania. Their circle of friends was made up of many in the scientific community, including Vladimir Zworykin, a physicist known for his work on the early television camera, and David Sarnoff of the Radio Corporation of America.[18]

Another regular at these gatherings was Alla's cousin, Sergei Sergeivitch Nekrassoff. A former White Russian soldier, Sergei escaped Russia in 1917 through Germany and France. He took a ship to Argentina and from there to New York. A skilled artisan, he developed a technique for enameling on copper and established a successful business in Connecticut producing decorative lamps, ornaments, and ashtrays that were sold in some of the better department stores. He moved his company, Nekrassoff and Son, to Stuart, Florida, and continued to produce art pieces until metal shortages in World War II forced him to close. In an interview Sergei's son recalled that the family had an ancestor in Russia who was occasionally mentioned as having been an outspoken advocate for peasants and serfs.[19] This may have been the popular nineteenth-century poet Nicolai Nekrassoff, who was disinherited for his beliefs by his father, an officer in the Imperial Army. Several things point to the possibility of this family link. One is that Nicolai, like Alla, was from Tula. Both fathers were high-ranking officers in the Imperial Army. Finally, Tania mentions in her diary that while sorting through old family belongings, she discovered a volume of poetry by Nekrassoff.[20]

Alla's mother and brother, Colonel Valvodya Alexandrovich Nekras-soff, were also present at family parties. Madame Nekrassova was a tiny aristocratic woman who fled Russia after the defeat of the White Army by the Bosheviks. She had survived the loss of her husband and home to the war and the revolution, as well as the loss of another son who had died earlier, while on a training mission in the Imperial Navy. In Lans-downe, she often sat doing needlepoint, chain-smoking, and speaking in Russian or French with her family and friends.[21]

In 1923 the household grew once again when Avenir sent for his youngest sister, twenty-eight-year-old Ludmila Proskouriakoff. "Mila," a talented artist who had a degree in architecture from an institute in Russia, hoped to continue her studies at the University of Pennsyl-vania, but she was not yet proficient in English. A friend of Avenir's, Wilbur K. Thomas, who served as secretary of the American Friends Service Committee from 1918 to 1929,[22] offered her a job in his office working the mimeograph machine while she improved her English skills. Mila married Paul Chenzoff, a Russian engineer who had grad-uated from Rensselaer Polytechnic Institute in New York. She and Tania developed a very close relationship and shared an interest in drawing. She was an important influence on the artistic development of her gifted niece.[23]

Tania, now called "Duchess" by her family and friends, was greatly stimulated by the environment at Lansdowne High School. She found a good friend in Josephine Suddards, a bright-eyed, curly-haired class-mate who lived just down the street. Both had a quick sense of humor and worked on the school yearbook, the *Garnet and Gray*. By their senior year, Tania was active on the debating team, editor-in-chief of the yearbook, and the class valedictorian. She thrived under the watch-ful eye of her teacher and adviser, Ms. Hall. Printed in the Personals section in the 1926 yearbook is the entry, "Don't give up hope, Tatiana, the teachers will soon learn." Another, reflecting her growing interest in architecture, exclaims, "Ah! Her Majesty approaches in scientific—no, not scientific but architectural—splendor! Who is this brilliant star of L.H.S.? We know she's the valedictorian, but here's some inside information: She fled with the rest of the nobility and is now trying

Lansdowne High School 1926 Yearbook staff, Lansdowne, Pennsylvania. Tania is seated fourth from the left, and her best friend, Jo Suddards (McCall), is fifth from the left. Photocopy from yearbook provided by Matthew Schultz.

to overthrow America by planning homes far from Killough's or McClatchy's idea of modern. Keep this latter quiet, for she may be seized."[24]

Tania's skills in sketching and painting in watercolors steadily improved as she practiced in her third-floor studio at home. She was now prepared to attend a university where she would receive training for the professional life she fully expected to lead.

CHAPTER THREE

Architecture at Penn State and Beyond (1926–1935)

Many of the young men in Lansdowne High School's graduating class of 1926 planned to attend the University of Pennsylvania. Most of the young women were bound for West Chester Normal School, where they would study to become teachers.[1] At this time Tania had no interest in teaching, and with her sights set on architecture, she and one other Lansdowne graduate planned to attend Pennsylvania State College. Financial matters figured in this decision.

Since the Proskouriakoffs were already paying Kay's tuition at Cornell University, they decided that Tania should make use of a fund that had been set up after the czar's abdication. Money that had once been allocated to pay for munitions was now available for loans to help Russians seeking degrees in the United States.[2] A 1925 catalog from Pennsylvania State College stated that an undergraduate could expect to spend from $500 to $800 a year for an education, depending on how frugally she lived.[3] Frugality appealed to Tania, and she was proud that she eventually paid back all the money borrowed from the fund for her education.[4]

The move from the metropolitan Philadelphia area, with almost two million people in the 1920s, to the rolling hills of rural central Pennsylvania was a tremendous change for Tania.[5] She no longer had the comfort of her family and close friends in Lansdowne or the varied cultural activities the city offered, but she was determined to establish a reputation as a serious student. In 1981 Tania told a friend that in choosing her major she did not wish to compete with Kay, who was pursuing a degree in chemistry. Mathematics and physics intrigued her, but at that time these disciplines usually led to teaching positions for women.[6] Penn State offered art history, interior decoration, painting, and drawing, as well as graphics courses, through the architecture department, and these interested her. With her usual energy when faced with a new challenge, she took on the demanding coursework in the architecture department, then part of the School of Engineering.

For students on many campuses across the United States, this was a period of great optimism and exhilaration. The depression that would hit in 1929 was unimaginable to the young women who attended classes with bobbed hair and short skirts. Jazz was the music that drove their dances, and Prohibition had done little to slow the tempo of their lifestyle. Although life at Penn State was subdued, it was still an exciting time to be a student there. A major building drive in the mid-1920s had resulted in construction of the women's dormitory, Grange Memorial Hall, Tania's final campus residence. Old Main, the original structure at the center of the campus, was being replaced by an attractive brick building that would provide space for students to have meetings and informal gatherings, as well as for administrative and alumni offices. College Avenue, bordering the Engineering Units where Tania took many of her classes, had recently been paved. And the Nittany Lion Inn, an elegant hotel and dining facility, was near completion. In June 1930 Tania's graduating class was the first to hold its commencement in the new Recreation Hall.[7]

During the 1920s, three-fourths of the five hundred women at Pennsylvania State College were enrolled in the School of Education, most of them studying home economics.[8] By studying architecture, Tania was choosing a path that clearly put her in the minority. A photograph in the 1927 college yearbook shows Tania sitting in the front row of the Architect's Club. She is the only woman among the twenty members. It was a role to which she would become increasingly accustomed over the years. It is important, however, that Tania rarely spoke about how her gender influenced her career. She simply chose a field of study and then gave it her best effort.[9] All her important female role models, her mother, aunt, and sister, had not shied away from male-dominated professions. Nor would she.

In her first year at school Tania continued her interest in debate and was one of two freshmen on the Girls' Debating Squad. She was developing her style of speaking, which later in life was considered combative by some, direct and challenging by others. Debate was one more way for Tania to continue sharpening her command of the English language. In her junior year she was named to the honorary fine arts fraternity, Pi Alpha Gamma, which was composed of a group of architecture students selected in their junior and senior years for outstanding work in the department. Also in that year she became a member of the scholastic club Phi Kappa Phi, and she received the prestigious John W. White Junior Scholarship, awarded to one outstanding student each year.[10]

One of the electives that Tania chose would prove highly valuable in her fieldwork. It was a course in surveying, offered through the School of Engineering. Tania later told a friend that the surveying class had required a final project and that most of the students had arrived at results quite different from her own. Though she feared she might fail the course, she stuck with her calculations. It turned out that hers were correct, and she completed the course successfully.[11] As she would throughout her life, she had set high standards for herself, demanding accuracy in her work and standing by her conclusions, even if they contradicted the findings of her colleagues.

It was during her college years that Tania first immersed herself in the study of the great impressionist painters, whose works she greatly admired. In 1946 she reflected in her diary, "How little I understood the significance of that period which so permeated my thoughts in my college days—and why indeed did that particular period have so much influence with me—surely there was material more modern in the twenties. Was it cultural lag?"[12] She also experienced periods of self-doubt and despondency, which continued to plague her periodically as an adult.

In a later diary, she wrote, "I have a vague and uncomfortable feeling that my life is unsatisfactory. Remembering my college doldrums when life was still ahead, I can only conclude that it is constitutional."[13]

In spite of this, it seems that Tania surrounded herself with fun-loving friends, some of whom came home with her to Lansdowne for vacation. Polly Margolf, a college friend, wrote, "[Tania's father] was a chemist who made his own Vodka. Her parents often entertained the 'gang' of architectural students; we ate, drank, and danced into the wee hours." Of a visit with her old friend nearly fifty years later, Margolf wrote, "All the years flew away, [she was the] same good friend, same charming person, same contagious giggle."[14] Tania's "doldrums" were not apparent to others.

One requirement for a bachelor of science degree in architecture was an internship with an architectural office as a drafter. In summer 1929, Tania went to New York City to interview. After being turned down by many firms, she was finally offered a job. However, she chose to work with Chapman Interiors, a firm in downtown Philadelphia, so that she could keep her expenses down by staying with her family. In 1981 Tania described that summer's work: "My first job there was to design murals for an office in a skyscraper which belonged to a water company, so I had Neptune coming out of the sea and all kinds of things about water." She explained that when her designs were incorporated into the build-ing, she was fascinated to find that measurements often changed as adjustments were made during construction. She concluded, "That helped me a lot in archaeology later on. I realized then that not only steel construction but also stone construction changes shape."[15]

With the stock market crash of October 1929 and the following eco-nomic instability, the unbounded optimism that many college students had felt during much of the decade, came to an end. Jobs of any sort were becoming more difficult to obtain. The architecture students in the Pennsylvania State College class of 1930 faced a harsh reality on grad-uating. In spite of their training and degrees, there was little work to be found in their chosen field. It would become far worse in the years ahead. Between one-fourth and one-third of all American workers would be unemployed by 1932.[16]

Tania graduated on June 10, 1930. In the Penn State yearbook section for her class of architects and architectural engineers, there is an attractive photograph of her. She is wearing a beret, and her eyes appear large, as she gazes to one side. She has a hint of a smile on her lips. The caption beneath the photograph notes that her major is architecture, that she is twenty years old, 5'3", and weighs 114 pounds, and that her preferred location is Philadelphia.[17] An important phase in her life was over, and another was about to begin. Tania had made her own way and had established a reputation for academic excellence in the male-dominated architecture department. She had made a circle of new friends, both male and female, and for the first time had "confronted the man/woman relationship,"[18] as she mentioned in a later diary.

Tania returned to Lansdowne, but there is scant record of her activities during the next five years. Her niece and nephew both believe that she had numerous marriage proposals in her life, and close inspection of a photograph from this time shows a ring on her left, fourth finger. However, even in her private diaries, which she began to keep at the age of thirty, Tania was often vague when writing about her relationships with men. Although there are notable exceptions in the late 1940s and the 1950s, she rarely included specific details, perhaps because these were personal reflections, not written for others. An example of such an entry is when her father told her that he had seen a Dr. Boyd at a recent scientific conference. Tania tantalizingly wrote, "It seems that he prospers . . . has no children and is fat and happy. . . . I suppose he has forgotten gardenias."[19] Around this same time, another entry mentioned that her mother had written her with news of old friends. Tania wrote moodily, "Igor has married?? I don't particularly like that either."[20] Though her private life during these years is sketchy, there are details that are known.

She worked briefly as a white-gloved salesgirl at an elegant department store, John Wanamaker's, in downtown Philadelphia. Now on the National Register of Historic Places, during the 1930s the store was known for its upscale merchandise. Its large, bronze sculpture of an eagle, which still greets shoppers, was a favorite meeting place for young people. Another part of the shopping experience that continues today is the tradition of daily concerts on an immense organ, whose

Proskouriakoff family photo, Lansdowne, Pennsylvania. Standing: Tania's father, Avenir (the Skipper). Seated left to right: Cassia, now called "Kay," Alla, Tania. Courtesy of Mike Beetem.

pipes dominate one side of a lavish seven-story atrium.[21] In 1949 Tania reflected on her experiences as a salesgirl, when she described a woman being fired from the office of the Carnegie Institution of Washington:

> The employer-employee relationship in our society is irremediably wrong; so fundamentally wrong that no economic or social reforms can overcome it; for a man who has power to deprive another of his joy has greater power than anyone should have over another. I saw it . . . when I was working at Wanamaker's and was appalled by the feeling of fear of being fired which poisoned the lives of all the salesgirls there.[22]

Fortunately, Tania found another job with less pressure, one that drew on her artistic skills. Sinkler's Studio, located on an old estate in Radnor

Tania. Courtesy of Mike Beetem.

along the Main Line, produced original needlepoint designs for Philadelphia's wealthier families. Mrs. Sinkler's husband had died during the
depression years, and with six young children to support, she began to
charge for her patterns. As few of her clients were affected by the eco-
nomic hardships around them, she was able to hire several women. The
women painted in light oils directly on each canvas, specifying the wool
to be used. Among her clients were members of the Dupont family and
the wife of the actor Claude Rains. Some came for the studio's designs
that were adapted from classical patterns. Others wanted personalized
designs, such as flowers, pets, and school seals to be put on pillows, rugs,
or servants' bell pulls. Many clients wished to have reproductions of their
large homes, and it was this last task for which Tania and her aunt Mila,
who had also begun working at the studio, were particularly well trained.

One woman who had once been employed at Sinkler's recalled that Mila, or "Madame C" as she was called, seemed stern and distant at first but warmed when asked for ways to improve a drawing. Another recounted that Mila spoke out loud to herself as she worked. When this was brought to her attention, she replied dryly, "Well, I like to talk with someone *intelligent!*"[23] Stories like this reveal that there was a comfortable camaraderie among the women who worked together in the bright studio. When a client requested a particularly demanding oriental design, Tania went to the University of Pennsylvania Museum to look at works in that style.[24] What she saw there began to capture Tania's lively mind.

She took several graduate courses at the University of Pennsylvania and competed for a position on an archaeological expedition to Mesopotamia under the auspices of the University of Pennsylvania Museum. Of the thirty students who applied for the position, only one, a senior from the university's School of Fine Arts, was selected. A local newspaper reported, "Men only will accompany the expedition, a fact which barred the participation of the one woman contestant, Tatiana Proskouriakoff, a graduate student and a Philadelphian who, though well qualified for the work, could not be accepted. . . . As qualification for the position it is said that the successful contestant must be one-third architect, one-third surveyor and one-third red-blooded American ready to meet all emergencies."[25] If she had been accepted, Tania would have set sail on December 10, 1930, for the Middle East. Instead, her journeys, still some years ahead, would take her in a different direction.

CHAPTER FOUR

Into the Jungle

The University of Pennsylvania Expeditions (1936–1938)

Late in her life, when a student asked Tania how she had become an expert in the Maya field, having taken no courses in archaeology, she replied that she had read every book on the subject in the University of Pennsylvania Library. When the student gasped in awe, Tania quickly continued, "Oh, it wasn't hard. That included only about six books at the time."[1] With published material on the Maya in the 1930s still quite limited, her statement is accurate, but it also illustrates Tania's dry sense of humor. As colleagues and students who knew her well noted, she was able to set others at ease with a humorous remark, never at anyone's expense but her own.

Of the books available to Tania in her early career, one of the most popular was *Incidents of Travel in Central America, Chiapas and Yucatán* by the nineteenth-century American explorer John Lloyd Stephens. Having found success with accounts of his travels in Egypt, Greece, and eastern Europe, Stephens turned his attention to the relatively unknown jungles of Central America.[2] Through a connection in the American government, he was appointed diplomatic agent to the new and poorly integrated Central American Confederation. Wisely, he persuaded the

English architect, Frederick Catherwood, to accompany him on his journey. When Stephens's account was published with Catherwood's illustrations of the forgotten temples and monuments they encountered, their book generated widespread interest in the region.

Later expeditions to the area in the nineteenth century by the German explorer Teobert Maler and the Englishman Alfred P. Maudslay produced a wealth of photographs of previously unknown archaeological sites with many intricately carved monuments. The academic world began to recognize the tremendous effort that would be required to understand such a complex civilization. By 1914 the energetic and charismatic American, Sylvanus G. Morley, who had studied under Alfred M. Tozzer at Harvard University, convinced the Carnegie Institution of Washington (CIW) to support annual expeditions into these remote areas. With his unfailing devotion to the modern Maya and his explorations of the region to record all monuments with calendar dates, Morley had a profound effect on the field. Over the years, he influenced many, Tania among them, to take up his cause.

The CIW supported two long-term excavations in Central America, both of which were producing exciting results. At Uaxactún, in the heart of the Petén, under the direction of Oliver G. Ricketson, dramatic discoveries were pushing the beginnings of the Maya civilization ever earlier. The second project, at Chichén Itzá in Yucatán, Mexico, was conceived and directed by Morley.[3] The restoration of the pyramid called El Castillo, which is visited each year by more than three million people, is one visible result of this wide-ranging project.

The University of Pennsylvania Museum soon initiated an archaeological project of its own in the Maya region. The university's commitment to archaeology was long established. In the late 1880s trustees of the university had sponsored an expedition to the Near East and provided funding for a building, now known as the University of Pennsylvania Museum, to accommodate any artifacts brought back. With international acclaim in 1895 for its excavations in present-day Iraq, the museum next turned its attention to the New World[4] by sending Henry Mercer to excavate caves in Yucatán in search of evidence of early man. While there, Mercer also visited the archaeological sites of

Uxmal and Kabah.[5] These sites would one day have special significance to Tania.

In 1930 aerial photographs from Charles Lindbergh's reconnaissance flight over the Maya region showed evidence of unmapped archaeological sites in the jungles below.[6] Recognizing the potential of aerial photography in archaeology, the museum sent Percy Madeira and J. Alden Mason, curator of the museum's American Section, on a similar flight. They too made new discoveries, which they later presented at the museum in a lecture, broadcast over WHAT Radio. Covering their recent Central American explorations, the lecture fueled public interest in the Maya region.[7]

In 1931, with input from Morley and Tulane University's Franz Blom, Mason chose the site of Piedras Negras for the museum's first long-term Maya project. Named for the black stones found along the shore of the Usumacinta River on the border between Mexico and Guatemala, Piedras Negras was chosen by Mason because of the quality and quantity of carved sculpture discovered there. The hieroglyphic texts on these sculptures led to Tania's breakthrough discoveries years later, forever linking her name with this site.

For the first expedition, Mason chose Linton Satterthwaite Jr. as his archaeological assistant, marking the start of Satterthwaite's lifelong commitment to the ancient Maya. Years after his death, a prominent scholar in the field described him as "one of the great unsung heroes of Maya epigraphy."[8] In 1933 he became project director, the position he held for the next six years until he was named a curator in the University of Pennsylvania Museum. He was the first person to recognize Tania's potential in Maya archaeology, and his impact on her life and career was profound.

Born in 1897, Satterthwaite was the second of four children. His father was a Yale-educated lawyer who had published articles on labor organization and reform and was active in the Democratic Party in Trenton, New Jersey. As the eldest son, Satterthwaite followed in his father's footsteps, attending Yale College[9] while both of his sisters studied at Swarthmore College. In September 1918, before completing his degree, he shocked his family by enlisting in the Royal Air Force in Canada.

With the hope of contributing to the war effort, he trained as a pilot and received a commission as second lieutenant. He was then sent to England, but the signing of the armistice on November 11, 1918, ended all hostilities before he saw combat. He returned to the United States to resume his studies and graduated with the Yale class of 1920.[10]

The air force training Satterthwaite received initially led him to consider a career in aircraft construction. Influenced by his father, he instead chose to study law, working part-time as a newspaper reporter from 1920 to 1923. He began to practice law in 1924, one year after the death of his father. This, he dutifully though unhappily continued to do for the next four years, but a growing interest soon took him in an entirely new direction. He began working as an archaeological assistant on a project in Pennsylvania, later on another in the Texas Panhandle. Next he worked on the excavation of an Indian mound at Beech Bottom in West Virginia, which resulted in his first publication with the University of Pennsylvania.

In 1930 Satterthwaite married Margaret Elizabeth Conway, a strong-willed young woman from Trenton. The couple quietly celebrated their first anniversary in the jungles of Guatemala. It was the first of many expeditions they shared in the course of their fifty-year marriage, although there were times in her life that Peggy wished Satterthwaite had remained a lawyer. In the archaeology community, they are fondly remembered for their generous support and gracious hospitality, both in the field and in their home. Tania was among the frequent guests at their parties for archaeologists setting out for Central America. At this time, she was still "a shy and retiring individual who didn't have much to say,"[11] although this would change dramatically as she grew in her profession.

During the early 1930s while working for Sinkler's studio, Tania began to volunteer at the University of Pennsylvania Museum, doing drafting work for the classics department in exchange for library privileges. Since the classics collection at the museum was exhibited in a gallery directly outside of Satterthwaite's office, he became aware of the delicate artistry and careful attention to detail in Tania's sketches. Learning that there was little work remaining for her with the classics department, Satterthwaite suggested she could begin to draw material gathered on the Piedras Negras expeditions. He set her to work at a large wooden drafting table in the room adjacent to his book-lined office. The table where she drew is there still, along with a small wooden chair with the initials "T.P." carved into the back.[12] So began a friendship that spanned four decades of change for both.

In 1936 Satterthwaite asked Tania to participate further in the Piedras Negras field project by drawing up plans of the architecture at the site. In a letter to Morley, Satterthwaite writes,

> The party will consist of Peggy and myself, Frank Cresson[,] . . . and in addition, Miss Tatiana Proskouriakoff, the graduate architect and artist who has been helping as a volunteer for about a year. She is the girl who drew the shell inscription so beautifully for me. While her main job will be making plans of buildings, if there is any time to spare I may start her on a job which has been in the back of my mind a good while. That is, I think all Piedras Negras sculpture should be carefully drawn to scale.[13]

This was a major crossroad in her life, and Tania accepted the job, although it paid only her travel and living expenses. With the United States still deep in the depression, budgets were tight everywhere. Even the venerable Carnegie Institution of Washington was unable to pay much more than this to the young architect John P. O'Neill when he was employed by Morley in Yucatán in 1932–33.[14] For her first expedition, the greatest expense Tania faced was the purchase of clothing she would need for travel and the months of rugged working conditions in the field.

Tania's greatest concern, however, was for the equipment she would use in making a survey of excavated buildings. To prepare, she practiced on a borrowed transit and carefully studied the instructions for replacing damaged hairs in the telescope. As she had anticipated, a tiny hair did break at a crucial time during the field season, and to repair it, she had to search the jungle for the finest spider web she could find. With a piece of the delicate web, she carefully replaced the transit hair.[15] Tania's perseverance and self-reliance were valuable qualities that she demonstrated often throughout her long career.

Tania with the Satterthwaites, awaiting transport en route to Piedras Negras, 1937. Courtesy of Mike Beetem.

In her diary, Peggy Satterthwaite described traveling by train in 1931 from Philadelphia to New Orleans, where passage on a boat was secured for crossing the Gulf of Mexico to the Yucatán Peninsula's port of Progreso.[16] Tania took the same route five years later, when the expedition included both Satterthwaites as well as a young man, Frank Cresson, who had signed on for the project. From Progreso, they went inland to the city of Mérida, from which they took a train to the colonial town of Campeche on the west coast. From there they sailed on a schooner overnight to Ciudad del Carmen, deck chairs on the front of the boat serving as their beds. In Carmen they boarded a riverboat that carried them more than three hundred kilometers inland. Along the way they saw spider monkeys and watched countless white egrets take flight from the overhanging trees. It was a new and exciting world for Tania.

They disembarked at Monte Cristo and hired mules for their ride overland to visit the ruins of Palenque. Tania later declared that it was here, on first seeing the elegant Temple of the Sun nestled in the lush rain forest, that she knew she had found her life's work.[17] She was not the first, nor would she be the last, visitor to be so moved by the grandeur of Palenque. Even today, as one of the premier destinations in Mexico, the beauty of these ruins and the surrounding forest is profoundly moving. For the members of the Piedras Negras expedition of 1936, but especially for Tania, who was seeing a Maya pyramid for the first time, Palenque made an indelible impression.

Returning to Monte Cristo, the group continued upriver to Tenosique, a small town on the Usumacinta River, where arrangements had been made for a large mule team and muleteers to meet them. Packed with the supplies and equipment needed for the field season, the mules carried them the remaining sixty-four kilometers overland to the site. They covered the same territory that a later Mayanist, David Stuart, would do in 1998, when he carried a small but precious container of ashes to be buried in Piedras Negras. The same route was cleared during one field season in the 1930s for transporting stelae out of the site for shipment to the United States. During this period, sometimes referred to as "museum archaeology," monuments were often removed from sites for exhibitions at major museums around the world.[18] Since then, Tania and

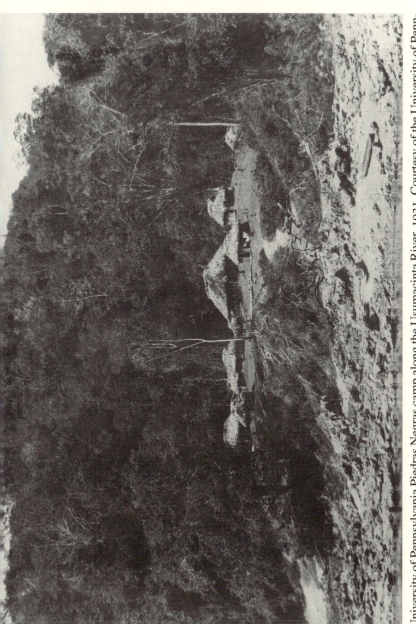

University of Pennsylvania Piedras Negras camp along the Usumacinta River, 1931. Courtesy of the University of Pennsylvania Museum, Philadelphia (NC 35-15506).

many of her colleagues in the field of Mesoamerican archaeology have supported passage of international laws to prevent antiquities from being removed from their country of origin. It was a deep concern for Tania late in her life and continues to be a concern for many today.

With several hours remaining before they would reach the site, Satterthwaite's crew stopped to set up camp for the night. As dusk settled on the jungle close around them, the air was filled with the roar of howler monkeys in the distance. This distinctive sound, frightening at first, became as familiar to Tania as the noises of the city she had left many weeks before. The next day, as the mule train approached the site, she saw the river through the trees and the rustic camp that would be their home for the next three months. In a cleared area near the river's edge, it consisted of thatched huts, a large one for dining and smaller ones for sleeping quarters. Tania settled into one of these alone, unpacking the trunks of clothing, equipment, and supplies she had brought along.

Camp routine was soon established. Breakfast was served early each morning by one of the staff, after which the party proceeded to the ruins to begin work. Satterthwaite set the schedule, overseeing excavations at the various temple groups. While surveying, Tania became convinced that a stairway would be found on a pyramid's side where Satterthwaite said there was none. He challenged her to prove her hypothesis and showed her how to proceed with the excavation. To her satisfaction, she found the evidence of a stairway where she dug, and Satterthwaite was brought around to her point of view.[19] This was not the last time she would challenge authority.

With mapping as her primary responsibility in the field, Tania needed to be extremely accurate when taking measurements. Carrying her transit and measuring tape, she worked diligently in rugged terrain. Toward the end of the season, however, she discovered that the cloth surveyor's tape had begun to stretch. When she measured it, she found that the first meter of the tape was off by five centimeters and each meter beyond that by several more. Based on how long she had been in the field, she formulated an adjustment to compensate for the cumulative error introduced in her drawings, a tedious but necessary task.[20]

Tania, measuring Structure J-11 at Piedras Negras, 1937. Courtesy of the University of Pennsylvania Museum, Philadelphia (S5 17233).

Satterthwaite was a highly disciplined and organized leader, but he also knew the importance of relaxation. For this reason, he made it part of the routine to clean up and change into suitable clothing for cocktails and dinner at the end of the long day. Tania often walked through mud on the trail from her quarters to the dining hut, wearing a long, white cotton dress, the evening attire Satterthwaite prescribed for both her and Peggy. Joining her and the Satterthwaites were Frank Cresson and Victor Pinelo, a Guatemalan government representative overseeing the work. After the hot, humid hours climbing about the ruins, Tania enjoyed the stimulating conversations and the cocktails served with smoked clams on Melba toast.[21] Such evenings were reminiscent of those she had enjoyed at her parents' house, where they frequently entertained lively intellectuals and Russian expatriates.

There were occasional guests. In 1936 J. Alden Mason came for an inspection visit. The next year, three CIW archaeologists arrived in the camp while on the final leg of a strenuous trip through the Petén. They were Edwin M. Shook, A. Ledyard Smith, and Harry E. D. Pol-

Piedras Negras. Left to right: Harry Pollock, Linton and Peggy Satterthwaite, Tania, Ledyard Smith, and Ed Shook, June 10, 1937. Courtesy of Dr. Edwin M. Shook.

lock, and each would later play an important role in Tania's life. Over evening cocktails, they told about a group of temples they had discovered at the remote site of Tikal. They shared stories about traveling by dugout down the Pasión and Usumacinta Rivers, of mapping the site of Altar de Sacrificios, and walking through the ruins of Yaxchilán. As they relaxed in the evenings, they also shared their discovery of two previously unmapped archaeological sites that they had encountered along the way. A warm camaraderie was common among Mesoamerican archaeologists in the field; they often visited each other's projects, shared their latest finds, and enjoyed animated discussions about the Maya.[22]

During each field season that she was at Piedras Negras, Peggy was in charge of bookkeeping and camp management. She oversaw the housekeeping staff and kept records of potsherds and other objects found by the excavators. Peggy enjoyed Tania's companionship and shared with her young friend the duty of ironing her husband's shirts, a task Tania later recalled fondly. Although work had initially brought them together, the friendship between these two very different women blossomed under the difficult conditions in the field and continued throughout their lives.

Satterthwaite's role as mentor to Tania evolved gradually over the years as she matured and began to excel in her profession. The early training he gave her in exacting fieldwork and thorough scholarship was invaluable in providing the solid base from which she developed. They had much in common. Both of their families had been influenced by the Quaker faith, and they both had strong ties to the Democratic Party. Their friendship was based on respect, humor, and intellectual stimulation, and it was enriched by the experiences they shared at Piedras Negras. Former students and colleagues describe both Tania and Satterthwaite as gracious, ethical, and generous with their expertise. But above all, their bond was based on a shared passion for truth, which each pursued in an effort to understand the ancient Maya and their complex writing system.[23]

At a time when Maya archaeology was made up predominantly of Ivy League men of independent means, Satterthwaite gave Tania her start, as he did even earlier to the ceramist Mary Butler. He had the ability to see talent and to nurture, encourage, and mold it in all those he met, regardless of gender. This farsightedness can be attributed in part to his upbringing in a family surrounded by strong, educated women. In a letter to Tania in 1943, he wrote, "Kidder told me you are permanently hooked to his [CIW] staff, which is good news for Mayaology."[24] It was, indeed, good news for Maya studies, though it would be some years before the truth of this statement would be widely recognized. While it was not Tania's direct intention, her career has served as an example to many women who have since chosen this profession. Today it is not uncommon for an archaeological project in Central America to have more women than men working together on an excavation.[25]

At the end of Tania's second field season at Piedras Negras, Satterthwaite and Peggy proceeded, with a Carnegie grant, to visit other archaeological sites in Guatemala and Honduras. Tania and Cresson traveled in the opposite direction, to visit the Carnegie project in Yucatán.[26] In a letter to Satterthwaite, she described this trip: "I was thoroughly scared on a pig-boat to Campeche, loved Mérida, was impressed with the monumental splendor of Chichén and Uxmal . . . and sailed home on the *Gatún*, quite enraptured with a calm and beautiful sea and lazy living."[27]

Back in Philadelphia, Tania delivered to the Academy of Natural Science forty-five insect specimens she had gathered in the jungle, some of which were previously unknown species.[28] She resumed her paying job with Sinkler's Studio and continued to work with Satterthwaite on a volunteer basis. In the room next to Satterthwaite's office, she completed the complex site map, begun in 1932 by Fred Parris and published in *Piedras Negras Archaeology*. This map has withstood the test of time and is still used by archaeologists at the site more than sixty years later,[29] although it does not show the location of the stelae that had such an impact on her later career. The drawings Tania made of the Acropolis at Piedras Negras would soon spark Sylvanus Morley's imagination and enthusiasm, and with his backing, Tania would embark on even greater adventures.

CHAPTER FIVE

Copán and the Carnegie Institution of Washington (1939)

While work on Piedras Negras continued in Philadelphia, Satterthwaite became increasingly disturbed that the straitened museum budget prevented him from offering Tania a salary for her meticulous drawings. He teased her by suggesting he was going to have to "fire" her. Years later Tania said that her response to this was, "Well, I may be fired, but may I have a desk here and some of your plans and drawings to work with? Because . . . here's this elaborate acropolis but you've got great piles of debris in every court and I can't see it. I can't form a very good picture of it . . . so I want to see if I can make a drawing from the plans and see what it looked like."[1]

It was in this challenging yet good-natured atmosphere that Tania produced her well-known reconstruction drawing of the Piedras Negras Acropolis. It was the first in her series of elegant renderings of Maya architecture, setting a standard of excellence artists and archaeologists still strive to match today.[2] Satterthwaite was pleased with the drawings and arranged for Morley to look them over while on a visit from Washington to the University Museum. Morley was always in search of new ways to increase the public's awareness and interest in this civilization,

Piedras Negras Acropolis. Original watercolor by Tania, housed at the University of Pennsylvania Museum Archives. Cour-

and he felt Tania's drawings had the potential to do just that. He wrote, "I believe Miss Proskouriakoff's architectural restorations give a better idea of how these ancient centers of the Maya Old Empire really looked in the heydays of their respective prosperity, than any other type of portraying them that has ever been made."[3] He asked if she would consider working for the CIW.

Founded by Andrew Carnegie in 1902, with an initial gift of $10 million, the Carnegie Institution of Washington was incorporated in 1904 by an act of Congress. Its purpose was "to encourage in the broadest and most liberal manner investigations, research and discovery, and the application of knowledge to the improvement of mankind."[4] Within ten years its endowment had more than doubled, and in 1914 when Morley received an appointment to the staff, the institution was spending nearly $1 million on research annually. Nine years with unstable political conditions in Mexico prevented Morley from starting the project for which he was hired. However, he began making yearly reconnaissance expeditions into the Maya region with the intention of establishing a definitive chronology for the Maya civilization. His emphasis on research and publication, rather than acquisition of artifacts, appealed to a growing sensitivity among many Latin Americans to their cultural heritage.[5]

Although there was no provision in the annual budget in 1938 for the work Morley was offering to Tania, he was not overly concerned. It was not unusual for him to raise funds on his own for particular projects, much to the chagrin of Carnegie officials. While still in Philadelphia, he was invited to a dinner party where the hostess, knowing Morley's propensity for fund-raising, requested only that he refrain from soliciting contributions until dessert was served. He graciously complied, and by the end of the party, he had gathered $500, enough to finance Tania's first Carnegie expedition. As Morley conceived it, Tania would travel to the heart of Central America, to the archaeological site of Copán in Honduras, where a large project was already under way.[6]

Wishing to look through the plans and drawings from Copán, Tania traveled to Cambridge, Massachusetts, to CIW's Division of Historical Research offices, which had been set up in an old house at 10 Frisbee Place, across the alley from the Peabody Museum at Harvard. Alfred

Vincent Kidder, a distinguished Harvard-educated archaeologist renowned for his work in the southwestern United States, had served as head of this division since 1929. He had recently moved the offices from Washington, D.C., to Cambridge, where many of his CIW research associates already made their homes.

Sitting across from Tania at his desk in a characteristically elegant suit, vest, and bowtie, Kidder was a formidable gentleman in his early fifties, with strong features, graying hair, and a moustache. Kidder was kind and often gave a sympathetic ear to the ideas of young archaeologists.[7] Over the years he made himself accessible to Tania, sharing with her his knowledge and wisdom and lending his support when needed. Of the matters they discussed that day in 1939, the most pressing was how Tania should make her way to Copán. She had received a formal letter from the director of the project, Gustav Strömsvik, welcoming her and asking her to bring along cartridges for making soda water. However, he gave no indication of how she should proceed to the site.

At first Kidder suggested traveling to Guatemala City where she could try to charter a small plane to fly her to the ruins. Uncertain how long it might take to find a pilot willing to make such a trip, he recommended instead that she book passage on a United Fruit Company boat out of Philadelphia bound for Puerto Barrios, Guatemala. By choosing this route, she could wire Strömsvik for the final directions to Copán and, while awaiting his directions, visit the ruins of Quiriguá, as Morley wished her to do.[8]

With her plans finalized, Tania returned home to Philadelphia and began packing in preparation for the expedition. There were the usual rounds of parties, and on February 13 she boarded the SS *San Gil* bound for Central America. The first day at sea was calm and cold. By that evening, near Cape Hatteras along the North Carolina coast, they sailed into a dense fog, slowing their progress considerably, and by the next day a large storm hit. In her diary, Tania wrote, "The sea is choppy[,] . . . turning into the biggest swells I ever saw, with white caps blown back by the wind. . . . [T]he wind is really terrific and spray is lashing against the portholes. The ship is shuddering and creaking. . . . This storm is getting worse toward night [with] lightning and rain and the ship tossing crazily around and blowing its whistle. . . . [H]ow I wish it would calm!"[9]

Tania's wish was granted. When the storm abated, she relaxed, enjoying calm, beautiful seas the rest of the trip. On passing the island of Cuba, she wrote, "It is the only point of interest today—except the flying fish, which skim over the water in all directions. But the blue of the ocean is so lovely that one cannot be bored watching it all day long. . . . I entertain myself by glyph calculations and radio. In the evening, we could see the Southern Cross."[10]

On February 20, one week after departing Philadelphia, the boat arrived at Puerto Barrios. Tania disembarked with her luggage and equipment and was met by the customs agent. Thinking the metal cartridges she had brought for Strömsvik were some type of bomb, the official detained her for questioning. When she protested that they were used for making soda water, he allowed her to keep the cartridges but to her great dismay, confiscated all her American cigarettes.

Agitated by this encounter, Tania found a room at the International Hotel, a dilapidated three-story wooden structure facing the water, with rooms opening onto a screened porch. It looked clean enough for the night, though she worried that the building easily could go up in flames.[11] The town had grown up on either side of railroad tracks, and the only store, a company commissary, carried canned goods and a few articles of clothing. In a letter to Mason, Tania described Barrios as "the most depressing town that I have ever seen."[12] The largely black population in town spoke English as often as Spanish, a comfort to Tania, who had not yet become fluent in the language.

After wiring Strömsvik of her arrival, she proceeded by train the next day to Quiriguá, which was located in the middle of a banana plantation owned and developed by the United Fruit Company. Ed and Wanda Clark, Americans who lived and worked there year-round, greeted her warmly. Their house near the company hospital served as a sort of tourist hotel. That day Tania wrote, "It is really a lovely spot, Quiriguá. The hospital looks beautifully neat and Ed's house . . . is spacious and cool and looks out on a beautiful lawn with palms and a gorgeous bread fruit tree."[13] Clark took Tania out to walk through the lush ruins, but she

Map of the Maya region, by Tania. Originally printed in the *Album of Maya Architecture*. Photo courtesy of Ian Graham.

found that the temples and monuments were badly overgrown with bush. She realized that to do the reconstruction drawings Morley wanted would require extensive clearing. Deciding to postpone her work there for a later date, she made arrangements to continue to Copán.

From Quiriguá, Guatemalan train service extended inland to the capital city. Tania traveled by train to the town of Zacapa, where she was able to catch a ride in a car, crammed in with eight others and all their baggage. They traveled over rough roads to the village of Chiquimula, where she took a room for the night at a small pension. In her diary she wrote,

> [The pension is] a single story building with a low tile roof, built around a tiny cobbled court that contains two small trees, a pump, a few small plants and half dozen chickens, not to mention a multitude of children. Marguerita Navarro y Lopez, six years old or so, is the only person here who can converse with me without any embarrassment, for my Spanish is simply atrocious. And she is simply adorable—even when she opens my toothpaste and insists it is for cleaning shoes."[14]

The next morning she hired a car to take her to Vado de Lela. The dirt road on which they drove was both terrifying and awe-inspiring:

> The mountains here are breathtaking, but the road is more than that. The men are either very courageous or just damn fools, for it's only by God's grace that we made it. The road is one car width and winds up the mountains by a series of hairpin turns. On the free side there is a sheer drop of some thousand feet and no banking, nothing to protect a skidding wheel. The cut made in the side of the mountain is vertical and who knows if a slide may be just around the bend.[15]

Strömsvik had wired that he had arranged to have mules waiting at Lela to carry her the last miles to the Carnegie headquarters in the village. When the driver arrived at this point on the Copán River, he stopped the car and put Tania's luggage and equipment out on the ground. Saying he could not miss a fiesta that evening in his village, he was about to leave her completely alone by the river with no mules,

house, or person in sight. She quickly suggested that he share her picnic lunch and insisted that if no one had appeared by the time they were
finished, she would return to Chiquimula with him. She later enjoyed
recounting, "Finally, just before he took off and while we were still argu-
ing about it, way up on a mountain was a little dot approaching, one guy
on a mule[,] . . . here was this young boy with a mule. He had come for
me, so I let the other men go."[16] The mule ride was a welcome change
for Tania: "It was a joy to be able to enjoy the scenery without praying.
I could not imagine anything to compare with it, this mass of mountains
that is Honduras. Pines above, palms below and mists floating between
the peaks. It is glorious, but I don't know if I should have knowingly
dared the venture."[17]

Arriving in the village, Tania walked into CIW headquarters in the
Casa Cuevas, home of one of the most important men of Copán, Don
Juan Cuevas. Situated at one corner of the main plaza, it was a large
stucco and tile-roofed house, part of which was reserved for the Cuevas
family, the rest for CIW staff. At the time, the staff included the project
director Strömsvik, ceramist John Longyear, and excavator Stanley
Boggs.[18] Tania described her arrival: "There was everybody assembled
at this huge table, which was filled with bottles and glasses, waiting for
me with champagne, whiskey and all kinds of things. The first thing
Gus said to me was, 'Did you get those cartridges?'"[19] She had brought
them, of course, but they were still with her trunks and equipment on
the other side of the river. He quickly sent someone out with mules to
retrieve them. This was Tania's first meeting with Strömsvik, and the
events of the evening set the stage for their relationship for many years
to come.

Tania sat down with the men for drinks, wishing to "chase away that
feeling of isolation and unreality." One of them suggested she could
join them in a friendly poker game, but she declined. She felt it would
be inappropriate since there were people from the village present who
did not yet know her. She went to settle into her room instead. She fell
deeply asleep but was awakened in the night by someone coming in
the door.

Knowing I had latched the door, I couldn't understand how he got there. Here was this Indian standing in front of me and gawking at me in the middle of my room. I looked at my clock and it said three o'clock. . . . [T]he only thing I could think of to say was, "Where is don Gustavo?" "Ay, se fué." "Where did he go?" . . . He made a drinking motion. He said, "I'm looking for Don Estebán." I didn't know who Don Estebán was, but it finally occurred to me it was Stanley Boggs, one of the crew. . . . Why he should be looking for Stanley Boggs in my room at 3 o'clock in the morning I couldn't quite understand. So it struck me as awfully funny and I started laughing, and he started laughing, and we were both almost doubled over with laughter, he standing there in front of me and me in bed. Finally, he explained to me that Gus was drunk and he had gone off to the monte and I had visions, having seen the terrain, of his falling into one of these barrancas. So I told him, "You go and look for him." And he said, "Oh, yes, we do that every Saturday night."[20]

Late in her life Tania told this story with genuine warmth and affection. While her relationship with Strömsvik began poorly, over the years it developed into one of the deepest and most important friendships in her life. At one time Tania considered writing his biography,[21] and the mention of his name brought a smile to her face as she whispered, "Ay, Gustavo, que buena gente."[22] Ah, Gus, such a good person. He was a complex and fascinating man who fell deeply in love with her, yet both remained single throughout their lives.

Gustav Strömsvik was born in about 1900 in Norway, the fourth of Ursella and Gustav Nikolai Strömsvik's six children. His father owned a small ship and made a living by transporting and selling fish. He fell ill and died in 1908, leaving his wife with no source of income. Ursella worked hard to keep the children together, but eventually she had to find homes for them with friends and relatives. Strömsvik went to live with a family in Tjongsfjord. At the age of twelve he left to work as a cook on a fishing trawler. He later became a sailor on a Norwegian tramp steamer traveling all over the world.

In the course of his travels, he became fluent in English, Spanish, French, and German.

In his early twenties, Strömsvik was working on a freighter as it sailed along the coast of Yucatán. Having grown tired of the poor food and a disagreeable captain, he and a friend jumped ship in the middle of the night and swam to shore. The next day, when they were not present for roll call, the captain notified the authorities that two men had been washed overboard. Locals discovered the body of a blue-eyed male matching his description, so they buried it, placing on the grave a small cross bearing Strömsvik's name. Years later, when out drinking in the nearby city of Mérida, he would drive with friends to the Progreso cemetery to place flowers on the grave and "to pray for the soul of Gustav Strömsvik."[23]

The night that Strömsvik and his companion swam ashore they headed inland to elude Mexican authorities. They found work at a sugar mill, earning a peso and a half per day. One day they read a report in the local newspaper about excavations being done by a group of Americans at the archaeological site of Chichén Itzá. Morley had finally been given permission to begin work on his long-awaited project for the Carnegie. The prospect of working with such a crew seemed most promising to Strömsvik and his friend, so they left the sugar mill and made their way to Chichén. Morley, an excellent judge of character, hired them immediately as handymen. Strömsvik proved invaluable, keeping things in repair and coming up with ingenious solutions to problems they encountered during the excavation. At the end of that first season, when Morley was leaving to return to the United States, he gave Strömsvik the job of caretaker of the project headquarters. This marked the beginning of his affiliation with the CIW, a diverse career spanning more than thirty years. Among Mesoamerican archaeologists, Strömsvik's story is legendary and is often recounted fondly.

In 1934, when an earthquake damaged Quiriguá, Strömsvik used his natural engineering skills to assist in the repair and replacement of stelae, some of which weigh up to sixty-five tons. When the Honduran government heard how effectively he carried out this work, they requested that he lead a similar repair project the next year at Copán. Kidder decided to expand the project to include excavation and mapping of the site and named Strömsvik director of the Carnegie project. Given the nature of the work to be done, he proved an outstanding choice.

During the field seasons before Tania's arrival, Strömsvik and Shook completed mapping the ruins of Copán. Strömsvik also designed a way to divert the flow of the Copán River so that it no longer eroded the base of the great Acropolis, an accomplishment that continues to benefit the preservation of the ruins to this day. For this project and for work at the site, he trained a crew of local men who remained deeply devoted to him over the years. He piped running water to the village from the surrounding hills and at the Carnegie headquarters constructed an outside shower stall and the first flush toilet in the region. For use in excavations at the ruins, he brought a pickup truck overland through rugged mountain passes where no road yet existed.[24] Colleagues like Shook and eventually Tania too, who had studied engineering in college, understood how valuable the practical skills were that came naturally to this man.

The day after arriving at Copán Tania requested a drawing table. Strömsvik ordered one to be built out of local cedar, then took Tania out for her first glimpse of the ruins. Although it was a chilly, rainy day, she was deeply impressed with what she saw. She wrote, "I feel again that the trip was worthwhile. Copán is magnificent!"[25] With a trained architect's eye, Tania fully appreciated the elegantly conceived plazas, soaring temples, and large, ornately carved sculpture of this classical Maya city. It has been recognized since the nineteenth century as a great treasure of Maya art and architecture. The enduring beauty of the ruins, nestled in the fertile Copán Valley, continues to impress the modern visitor, novice and expert alike.

In his field notebook, Strömsvik wrote, "We made a round of introduction starting with the Great Court and ending on top of Temple #1 where we sat for quite a while discussing various problems."[26] The next day Tania began photographing and making preliminary sketches of the ballcourt in the Main Plaza. As she described it, "My first task is the Copán ballcourt, and, simple as it seemed, it is already presenting difficulties. In drawing up Shook's plans, I find several inconsistencies,

—51—

COPÁN AND THE CARNEGIE INSTITUTION

The Acropolis at Copán, by Tania. Original drawing at the Peabody Museum of Anthropology and Ethnology, Harvard Uni-

and since the buildings have mostly been filled up with rubbish since their excavation, it's fairly difficult to check."[27]

That Sunday, typically a day of rest for the crew, Strömsvik wrote, "I think we could all stand getting out from Copán once in a while."[28] With this thought, he led a trip into the bush on mules in search of more ruins. Using an 8mm camera, John Longyear shot footage of the excursion, which shows the group riding on a narrow trail through the hilly terrain, stopping for refreshment at a remote thatched hut. Tania appears relaxed in riding pants and a long-sleeved white shirt, a bandanna around her neck, and a high-peaked straw hat on her head.[29] She later wrote, "The ride was fun, but I am scared of galloping on a mule and can't keep my seat!"[30] It was an excellent way for Strömsvik to assess the character of the woman who had been sent to work with his project.

Several days after this outing, Tania confronted Strömsvik with her misgivings about the ballcourt plan: "I finally got the courage to broach the subject. . . . [H]e seemed very much offended that I should presume to criticize his survey, and I wasted a good deal of time rechecking my impressions."[31] This entry suggests tension was building between the two of them, and in a pattern that repeated itself over the years he responded by drinking more heavily. For example, "Today, Gus is still drinking and hardly able to stand on his feet. . . . [T]his state of things rather disconcerts me." In addition, Tania began to have a fever that spiked each afternoon, leaving her irritable and fatigued. She wrote, "I am taking 20 grams of quinine today to see if it may be a touch of malaria. I should rather have it than pneumonia or TB, but whatever it is, it is a nuisance."[32]

A guest provided some relief from the increasing tension. He was an entomologist from the University of Utah who had come to gather black widow spiders and other specimens in the ruins. Hearing of his interest in spiders, the children of the village began turning up with dozens of tarantulas, which he dutifully purchased. To Tania's amusement, this inspired the children to bring even more spiders, as well as snakes, iguanas, and even a wild turkey to sell. She wrote, "Gringos buy all sorts of queer things!"[33]

George Roosevelt, an attractive young American Tania had been hearing much about, now returned to Copán. Although he was not officially on the staff, his family, from Oyster Bay, New York, had connections at the Carnegie Institution. Rumors circulated that he had been sent to Central America to keep him out of trouble in New York. He was friendly, fun loving, and energetic, and the staff was happy to see him return from his trip to San Salvador.[34] Though she found Roosevelt charming, Tania wrote, "His arrival has been just one more excuse to waste time. This is, of all places I know, the most difficult to work in. There is always some interruption or some celebration. . . . At 2:30 A.M., I was favored with a serenade—a guitar, a mandolin and at least a dozen drunks."[35]

Work now focused on the completion of the archaeological museum that was to be ready to coincide with the dedication ceremony for the opening of the road to Santa Rita. Once the cement walls of the museum were finished, Strömsvik began to chisel freehand the official coat of arms of Honduras over the entrance. On the day of the ceremony, dignitaries arrived from both the Guatemalan and the Honduran governments. Speeches and toasts were made while a band played. Among the crowds, as seen in Longyear's film, Tania sat with several other women in the shade on a grassy hill. She was casually elegant in a black and white belted dress and a brown felt hat, smoking an ever-present cigarette.

One of Tania's diary entries at this time suggests a shift in her relationship with Strömsvik: "I can't make out whether Gus' ridiculous proposition was made in earnest or with an ulterior purpose. Some things he said rather disturbed me and made me wonder if I haven't hitherto taken too much for granted [concerning] the integrity of my colleagues. At any rate, his saying them alone makes things very difficult for me here, and whatever reaction he expected I have no idea."[36] Shook, a lifelong friend of both, wrote in his memoirs that Strömsvik loved Tania but that he only had the courage to tell her when he was drunk.[37] It was an awkward and confusing situation for Tania, one that continued to disturb her in the coming years.

Her persistent fever and cough worried her as well, and morale among much of the crew appeared to reach a low point by late March. She wrote, "I am appalled to think how little I have accomplished since being here. . . . [W]hy do I waste so many hours in hesitation?"[38] She had questions concerning several of the temples she was supposed to be drawing, and other than being given free rein to dig in order to clarify points, she was getting few suggestions. In a lengthy letter to Satterthwaite, she wrote, "Information seeps out of Gus slowly drop by drop and mostly I have to make my own guesses as to the evidence on which the rebuilding of Copán progresses."[39] She worried about the accuracy of the terracing in her restoration drawing of Structure 11, and in her diary she wrote, "I am digging into Structure 26 a little too deeply and am confused with early stuff popping up in the most unexpected places."[40]

She was also concerned that whole sections of stone were being incorrectly placed in the fifty-foot-wide hieroglyphic stairway leading to the top of Temple 26. The stairway had collapsed in the 1800s, leaving a jumbled pile of carved stones that the Carnegie project was attempting to reconstruct. In her diary, Tania confided, "I'm afraid that what is being built up here is going to be a great puzzle someday to someone. That it's a puzzle to me now is a secondary matter."[41]

Archaeologists have since determined that the text gives the dynastic history of Copán, but because so few of the glyphs were deciphered at the time, Strömsvik's work at Copán continues to be respected. The Copán Mosaics Project, which is currently ongoing, uses great care in unscrambling the text and protecting the glyphs from further deterioration caused by groundwater and weather conditions.

In early April Kidder wired that he and his wife would soon make an inspection visit. This was timely as Strömsvik had been on a binge for several days during which he had wrapped himself in a blanket in the Carnegie office drinking beer. Tania wrote, "Once he even stumbled to my door in the evening and wanted to get in. I hate it here when things like that go on and sometimes I am even frightened of Gus. He isn't human when he's tight." He pulled himself together respectably for the Kidder's visit, and Tania later continued, "We have had a lot of fun since, for everyone has been sober to date and sticking to his job."[42]

A woman who accompanied the Kidders also helped to lift Tania's spirits. Anna Shepard, a dedicated ceramist, had been with the Laboratory of Anthropology in Santa Fe, New Mexico, since 1931, working often on ceramic analyses for the Carnegie. Shepard was made a full

Carnegie staff member in 1937, and she and Kidder worked closely together. As Shook described in his memoirs, she regularly worked "twelve, fourteen, fifteen hours without stopping, and she expected the people working with her to do the same thing."[43] At Copán Tania joined Shepard on her early-morning walks before breakfast. Tania wrote, "It is remarkably beautiful country and so varied that it is never tiresome to look at it. . . . Anna is good to talk to and I am a little ashamed of how much I did talk with her. . . . I hated to see her go this morning."[44] They discovered they had much in common. Both were single women working in a predominantly male field, and both were very close to their chemist fathers. Both favored an analytic, scientific approach to their work that was at odds with the more intuitive methods employed by some archaeologists of the day. Both women pursued interests in a wide range of subjects such as physics, mathematics, and philosophy and above all had "an inherent desire to get at the truth of the matter."[45] The two women decided to travel together from Guatemala City at the end of the field season.

In a letter to Mason, Tania wrote that on her return, she hoped to stop in Quiriguá again. But she added, "I doubt I shall, for I am finding lots to keep me busy here at Copán, where I can spend the rest of my life sketching stones and trying to fit them together into sensible designs."[46] Tania felt she needed to wrap things up with her drawings and confided in a letter to Satterthwaite, "I can't make up my mind whether I am having a hell of a good time or a hell of a time here. I love the place and am almost as fond of the ruins as I am of P.N. [Piedras Negras]. I wish that I could make the ruins look on a picture as grand as I imagine them!"[47]

During these final days, she had to confront Strömsvik with a mistake she detected in his reconstruction of Structure 11: "It was unfortunate that I had to be the one to point it out to him, for it makes my position here more difficult than ever, and because I feel guilty about it I have to forgive him for past sins. Still, it is no excuse for his propositioning me for the fourth time. I wonder why I haven't the heart or the courage to tell him off more vehemently."[48] In the context of the times, it is not unusual that Tania chose not to confront Strömsvik about his behavior toward her when they were alone. Though this would change as their friendship evolved, at Copán it was far easier for her to communicate with him on a professional than on an emotional level.

In spite of her misgivings about her own accomplishments during the field season, by the time Tania arrived in Guatemala City, her spirits had begun to lift. While staying at the Pensión Gerault, her temperature again returned to normal. Comforted by running water and a hot bath, her dark mood eased, and in her diary she wrote, "I did hate to leave Copán. . . . I am fond of the crowd there."[49] She spent the next day resting, shopping, and visiting the Museo Nacional, where she was particularly interested in the pottery of Uaxactún. She had more than a week ahead of her to travel and unwind before catching her boat home.

She left Guatemala City by bus early the next morning, passing through beautiful mountains en route to Panajachel, where she found a room at a hotel on the shore of Lake Atitlán. From her window she could see the picturesque lake surrounded by volcanoes in the afternoon haze. As she would often do in the years to come, Tania enjoyed the cool air and lingered outside at the water's edge to do some sketching. That evening, in the dining room, she overheard conversations in German, Spanish, and English, and in her diary she wrote, "I am getting too used to traveling alone to feel lonesome."[50] After a short but restful visit, she returned to Guatemala City to meet Shepard.

Together the two friends caught a plane for Cobán, the principal town in the mountainous Verapaz region northeast of Guatemala City.[51] Tania wrote, "From the air, the country is appalling. . . . I was, of course, as usual scared and thrilled in the plane. At times it seemed as if we would graze the tops of the ridges we crossed and then suddenly the land seemed to fall away for many miles."[52] Heavily settled by Germans during the nineteenth-century coffee boom, this mountainous region supports lush coffee plantations. While staying at a hotel managed by a German, the two women were invited to view an extensive collection of highland pottery owned by Edwin Wieseldorff, a prominent citizen of the town. In this tranquil setting there was little to suggest that within several years, World War II would radically change the lives of this German segment of the Guatemalan population.

From Cobán, Tania and Shepard were able to get a bus to the village of San Pedro Carcha where they hoped to find Mary Butler, the University of Pennsylvania ceramist who was conducting a survey in the area. Butler was several years older than Tania and had done her undergraduate work at Vassar, had completed her master's degree at Radcliffe, and was working on her Ph.D. Like Tania, she had worked under the supervision of Satterthwaite at Piedras Negras.[53] They found her "standing by a rustic bridge, waiting for her diggers to arrive." She seemed to Tania to be content with "her solitary life in the village, digging with enthusiasm on surrounding hills for potsherds."[54] The three women browsed through the Indian market in the village, and Tania splurged on several pieces of silver jewelry. By late afternoon Tania and Shepard returned to their rooms in Cobán to rest and prepare for the final leg of their journey.

Early in the morning they caught a ride in a truck to a railroad crossing where they boarded a train heading to the coast. At Panzos they stayed in a small guest house run by the railroad company and for their meals, walked a half mile to the village where Señora Leonardo prepared them dinner and boxed meals for the next day's river trip. After a restful sleep, they boarded a launch on the Río Polochic. These last ninety miles to the coast town of Livingston were entirely by water, a pleasure for Tania as they reminded her of happy days spent boating and fishing with her father, whom she fondly called "the Skipper." This was the most breathtaking part of their trip, and on the riverbanks they saw caimans and a great variety of water birds as well as monkeys in the overhanging trees. Crossing Guatemala's largest lake, Izabal, the captain navigated his boat to the Río Dulce, passing through a spectacular gorge with white limestone cliffs and lush tropical vegetation. By late afternoon they arrived in Livingston. To cross the bay to Puerto Barrios, they were told it would cost $8 to hire a boat, so they decided to stay the night and take the local boat in the morning.

By the time they arrived in Puerto Barrios, Tania had completed a large loop begun three months earlier when she first landed there on her way to Copán. She had time before sailing to take the train back to Quiriguá, fulfilling her promise to Morley. She found it "as charming as before"[55] and again enjoyed the hospitality of the Clarks. Tania hired several men who cleared and dug around the ballcourt, where they found, as Tania reported, "exactly nothing at all."[56] Clark guided her to several nearby mounds where she took measurements and made notes. With this brief job completed, she returned to Puerto Barrios.

On May 8 Tania boarded the *Castillo*, bound for the United States.[57] This marked the end of her first trip to Latin America for the CIW. There would be countless more trips in the years ahead, though none as memorable for Tania. She had worked with and eventually befriended one of the more colorful characters in the field, and although there had been difficult times for her emotionally, it was this expedition she most enjoyed recounting later in her life. However, as Tania sailed north on calm seas, events already taking place in Europe would soon dramatically change all she knew and loved.

CHAPTER SIX

The War Years (1940–1944)

Over the years the transition from Tania's seasons of fieldwork in Central America to office work in Cambridge would become a familiar experience. She learned to adjust to the contrast in climates and cultures and to working in a close office space after being outdoors much of her field season. Summer 1939 held more adjustments than other years, as Tania moved away from her family and friends in Philadelphia to an apartment near Harvard Square. In a letter to Mason, she wrote, "Although I intended to finish my job . . . and return to Philadelphia, the Carnegie people have asked me to stay on to do some perspectives of Uaxactún until December or January when Dr. Morley wants me to join him at Chichén to make views of that site." Satterthwaite had notified her that funds might soon be available for some drafting work, and concerned about letting him down, she continued, "I am sure he can easily find someone adequate. Aubrey Trik, I understand, has been without a job since he left Carnegie . . . and from what I've seen of his drawings, I'm sure he'd do it very well."[1]

One day during her lunch break in Harvard Square, Tania ran into Ed Shook at the Harvard Coop bookstore. He suggested that in addition to her field notebooks she keep a diary to record her reflections. Tania bought a small book, the first of many, and began describing her unease at the events taking place across the Atlantic: "I am working on perspective drawings of Str. A–V Uaxactún—at the moment rather halfheartedly. In Europe, war between England and France and Poland and Germany seems to be actually underway. In America, people are glued to their radios and are again beginning to say that Germans (Hitler) are capable of any atrocity."[2]

In the evenings Tania went out to dinner and the movies with Strömsvik and Stanley Boggs or visited the Shooks, where the group would play cards and listen to the nightly broadcast of "Information Please." When she was alone in her apartment, she worked on glyphs and read books on a variety of topics, often several simultaneously. These included works on the Maya, such as Morley's *Inscriptions of Peten*, and fiction, such as Steinbeck's *Tortilla Flat* or Conrad's *Lord Jim*. She also read professional journals and magazines like the *New Republic*.[3]

Tania's relationship with Strömsvik continued as well and left her often feeling ambivalent and uncomfortable. In her diary she confided, "Another evening with Stanley and Gus—not a very successful one. Gustav was glum. I was glum too for I promised myself not to go to the movies with him this week. There are several good reasons beside the fact that the routine entertainment is getting somewhat monotonous."[4] In another entry, she wrote, "In spite of my good resolutions, I spent the afternoon at a gangster movie with Gustav and later proceed to get quite tight on two Tom Collins, quite an achievement under ordinary circumstances. But it only goes to prove that at the moment I am bored and feeling a bit uprooted from my ordinary course of life."[5] And another: "I do sincerely like Gustav, but sometimes I feel that I'm not being strictly fair—in fact that I am at heart a cad. That knowing so certainly how trivial our relations always shall be—I ought not to allow even his transient feelings to be involved."[6] The unresolved relationship with Strömsvik, the temporary nature of her work with the Carnegie Institution, and the dramatic world events all contributed to a profound sense of restlessness.

Of the international crisis, she wrote, "Russia seems to have announced her intentions to enter Polish Ukraine. . . . I wonder how it would be to be of 'enemy' ancestry. For I assume that such a step makes Russia a belligerent in the war and though America is 'neutral' there is no doubt at all that she is on one side. The hissing that is heard in theatres when pictures of Germans are shown on the screen is reminiscent of past times."[7]

Harry Pollock, one of the Carnegie archaeologists she met at Piedras Negras, also invited her out, and she later described it as "a pleasant dinner . . . talking mostly of Archaeology." But politics were never far from her thoughts: "The situation in Europe however crops up spontaneously in almost every conversation. The assassination of the Romanian premier and the following executions are the headlines of the day, and in every restaurant, on every street corner, anywhere that one catches stray words, Hitler's is the name most mentioned."[8]

At work, Tania had completed her drawings of Uaxactún and was beginning sketches of a fountain she was asked to design for the central plaza in the village of Copán. In her diary she related the details of an important meeting with Kidder: "[H]e proposed that after the Chichén trip I might settle permanently as draftsman for C.I. [Carnegie Institution]—salary $1500. It seems quite low—but it is interesting work and a nice outfit and as secure as anything in the Maya field."[9] Undecided about whether linking herself permanently with CIW would be the best move for her career, she hoped soon to discuss the prospect with her father and Satterthwaite, the two people whose opinions she most valued.

She made plans for a short trip to Philadelphia in mid-October where she hoped to give a party for some friends who would soon be leaving for Central America. Conflicted about taking time off when she still had work to finish, she finally concluded, "[H]ome parties are rare these days and I have a yen to see my Philadelphia friends."[10]

It was Tania's father who among her family showed the greatest interest in her work. The two had always shared a strong bond, and she felt deeper acceptance and love from him than from anyone else in her life. In the thoroughness of her work, she emulated his devotion to scholarship. They also shared a love for boating and fishing on vacations at the family's cottage at Spray Beach, New Jersey, and at their rustic "camp" on Lake Winnepesaukee, New Hampshire. As girls, Tania and Kay had split their summers with family and friends at the shore east of Philadelphia and their camp on the large New England lake. In later years Kay often drove her children from their home in upstate New York to join the family. The cottage, midway between the bay and the ocean, allowed the Skipper ready access to his sailboat, *Lightning*, docked at the local yacht club. Boating was a part of the Proskouriakoffs' getaway in New Hampshire as well, as the only access to their camp on Bear Island was by water.[11]

The Skipper's interest in the Maya grew out of his pride in his daughter's work. Tania expressed the pleasure this gave her: "Today, looking through old letters I came across one of the Skipper's that he wrote me while I was in Copán. I wish he would write oftener—in spite of the disgraceful spelling and odd phrasing, his letters are always entertaining and often a little inspiring. . . . [S]ince he has 'discovered' the Maya and realized what keeps me pecking at them, his few words are a great lift."[12]

Having cleared her party plans with her parents, Tania notified Satterthwaite. She soon received a letter from him saying there was work she could do while visiting home, an arrangement that would be repeated periodically over the years. She agreed to ride to Philadelphia with Strömsvik, taking in the fall colors of New England on the longer, more scenic route over the Bear Mountain Bridge. On the morning of their departure, however, Strömsvik arrived several hours late. He had a bad hangover, so Tania drove most of the way and found the trip rather grim. Fully recovered and contrite, Strömsvik attended Tania's party the next night at her family's home, along with Aubrey Trik, the Shooks, and the Satterthwaites. The party was a great success, and in 1997 Shook still fondly remembered the special treatment the Proskouriakoffs afforded their guests.[14] It was an opportunity for Tania to return the hospitality she had enjoyed at her friends' homes, giving them the sort of sendoff she had often experienced herself.

While in Philadelphia, Tania attended a class Satterthwaite was teaching, "Introduction to the Archaeology of Middle America." At the museum she gathered the material he wanted her to draw, intending to work on it during her spare time in Cambridge. She also met with Tilghman Kennedy of the CIW who informed her that Morley was expecting her to make drawings at several sites in addition to those he had already proposed at Chichén and Uxmal. She requested another month to prepare for this extra fieldwork and finished her vacation in a flurry of parties thrown for her by family and friends.

Back in Cambridge, she wrote, "[I]t has been . . . so nice to be again with Mother and the Skipper and to feel that I still have a 'home' there. I have missed my friends—seeing them all again makes my life in Cambridge seem rather dull and cold. . . . [T]he two weeks seem very short and gay."[15] She threw herself into her work and resumed her lunches in Harvard Square with Ruppert and Boggs. She spent evenings reading, working on Satterthwaite's drawings, and occasionally joining her neighbors for a hand of bridge and the nightly radio broadcasts.

She prepared for her upcoming season in Yucatán by pouring over the extensive photographs on file at the Carnegie office and next door at the Peabody Museum. She made maps of Chichén and small sketches "to determine best points of view" for her final drawings. She felt "rather appalled by the amount of material yet to be covered" and, not having gotten far with her drawings for Satterthwaite, was "having qualms of conscience."[16] She began staying after hours to finish the drawings while still devoting regular office time to field preparation. She bought a new Rolleicord camera with a special lens and shot a roll of film to make sure she would be comfortable with it in the field.

With the war in Europe escalating, Tania feared this could be her final expedition to Central America. Her fears were justified. For more than a century, there had been strong economic ties between the region and Germany. In spite of Franklin Roosevelt's successes with his Good Neighbor Policy and, in 1936, his presence at the first Inter-American Conference for the Maintenance of Peace, popular sentiment in Mexico generally supported Germany. By 1940, however, Ávila Camacho, the newly elected president of Mexico, made it clear that his government would stand firmly with the United States. Initiated before the war by British intelligence in Guatemala, blacklists of businesses and families having connections with Germany were being updated and made available to American government agencies. These lists were later key to efforts to stop the flow of money and goods from Mexico and Central America into Germany.[17]

By February Tania was prepared to join Morley at Chichén Itzá. The hacienda once owned by the American archaeologist Edward H. Thompson had served as Morley's fieldwork headquarters since 1924. Outbuildings had been constructed to house the staff, and everyone gathered each evening at the Casa Principal for a sumptuous dinner prepared by Morley's Korean cook, Jimmy Chan. The number of people present varied nightly, as Morley opened his door regularly to visiting scholars and other travelers stopping at Chichén. Everyone dressed for dinner, "the men in white linen, shirt and tie; the ladies in dinner dresses."[18]

By the time of this 1940 trip, however, the CIW had completed its large project, and only Tania, Morley, and his wife, Frances, were present. They settled comfortably into bungalows at the Mayaland, property that bordered the ruins and was being developed by a Mexican named Fernando Barbachano.[19] Tania was able to spend her days drawing as Morley had intended. She worked on a view of Chichén from the north, including the Sacred Cenote, which was to figure prominently in her later career. Of the drawings she completed, this view of Chichén would become one of her most famous renderings and is included in her *Album of Maya Architecture*. This and other drawings of Tania's have since been used in countless publications, and it is for these and her later writings that she is well known.

When Tania completed her work at Chichén, she left for Mérida. From there she traveled inland with the Morleys to Uxmal, the largest of the ancient Maya cities in the hilly region known as the Puuc, which lies in the interior of the otherwise flat Yucatán Peninsula. With some of the richest soil on the peninsula, the Maya have farmed the Puuc zone extensively. To overcome the chronic shortage of water, they had constructed underground cisterns to collect rainwater.[20] Approaching Uxmal on the present-day highway from Mérida, the Pyramid of the Magicians can be seen from a distance. Tania's visit to these elegant ruins at the end of her field season in 1937 had left a deep impression on her, and

Tania's watercolor of the Hacienda at Chichén Itzá, in the office of Ian Graham, Peabody Museum. Courtesy of Ian Graham.

The Red House at Chichén Itzá, by Tania, at the Peabody Museum, Harvard University. Courtesy of President & Fellows of Harvard College, Peabody Museum, Harvard University (N 28438).

now, three years later, she was returning to produce reconstruction drawings of the ruins for the CIW.

She found her room at the archaeologists' house agreeable, with a concierge helping to arrange her things and bringing her potable water and tortillas. With the assistance of one worker she began taking the measurements needed for her drawings of the Monjas group and the Governor's Palace. Tania next hired a Mexican guide, Hector Arana, to take her farther into the region, to Kabah, Sayil, and Labna. Although today a paved two-lane highway passes within view of these sites, in 1940 the trip was slow and arduous through low, dense brush and over rugged dirt roads pocked with outcrops of bone-jarring rock.

In May the heat and high humidity in Yucatán are intense. Often, dark clouds gather in the distance, with a promise of rain that will not fall for another month. Along the narrow trails through the ruins, the parched underbrush is gray-brown and infested with tiny black ticks the size of a pinhead called pinolillas, which attach themselves to the legs of unsuspecting passersby. Rattlesnakes and coral snakes, scorpions, and stinging ants are common in the area.[21] In spite of these conditions, Tania got to each of the sites Morley had requested, taking the measurements necessary for the reconstruction drawings she would complete back at the Carnegie offices in Cambridge.

Years later Tania's colleague, Ian Graham, famous for his explorations in the rugged Petén region of Guatemala, wondered how Tania had endured the adverse conditions in the field.[22] In 1980, responding to a relative's inquiry, she wrote, "When I first started out as an archaeologist, it was great fun riding through the forest on muleback and digging in the ruins. Nobody then knew much about them, and, better yet, nobody except the group I worked with knew about me."[23] At another time, Tania wrote about her reaction to Louis Halle's book, *River of Ruins*, in which he describes a rugged journey through remote areas of Guatemala and Mexico where she too had traveled. She mused, "Had he ended the book with, 'Well, anyway, most of it was fun,' it would be a true story."[24]

Returning to the United States at the end of this field season, she was quickly brought back to the realities of the war in Europe from which she had been insulated during the previous months. She wrote, "Everything looks very ominous. I left a neutral country, but I came back to one with a leg over the fence. I have a feeling that only our unpreparedness now keeps us out of the fray." Later, she added, "[T]here is great agitation for armament and 'defense.' Even greater for investigation of foreign agents and . . . the right to 'tap wires.'"[25]

The "lunch club" resumed with Ruppert and Boggs at the Window Shop or "at the cheapest possible" restaurant in Harvard Square where their conversations focused on the Maya and the war.[26] Tania used quiet evenings at home to expand her overall understanding of the Maya by reading Alfred Tozzer's annotated translation of *Relación de las cosas de Yucatán*, written in the sixteenth century by Diego de Landa, a Catholic bishop, who in his religious zeal had burned countless sacred books of the Maya. The *Relación* contains vivid descriptions of daily life in Yucatán at the time of the Spanish conquest. Tania was also working earnestly with glyphs. She decided, however, to put this study off until she had brushed up on astronomy.[27]

Soon after her return Tania caught the overnight bus to New York and from there to Philadelphia for a visit with her family. Her sister had written that she and her family were moving to Oregon from upstate New York, and she wanted to get everyone together before leaving. It was a quick weekend visit, one that left Tania thoughtful about her relationship with her older sister: "Kay seems quite contented and, as usual, remote. I am rather embarrassed by any show of affection from her, for it seems to come from such a distance. . . . [T]hen, as usual, too, there are conflicts between Kay and the Skipper."[28] The family gathered to take photographs in the yard, and Sunday was busy with visits from old friends. This would be their final reunion. The next two years forever changed their family and the world around them.

At the Carnegie office, Tania continued her reconstruction drawings of Kabah, conferring with Harry Pollock, the archaeologist most familiar with the architecture of this region. He showed her an earlier photograph of the palace taken by Herbert Spinden in which three masks on the upper facade could be seen rather than the two she had drawn. She

Tania with her nephew, Mike Beetem, undated. Courtesy of Mike Beetem.

recognized that his criticism was valid but wrote, "I am redrawing the Kabah palace on which I have pulled a bad boner. . . . [S]eems I have done a sloppy job this year. Altogether I miss Linton's encouragement and inspiration."[29]

Tania began to express a deepening restlessness in her diary, a feeling that intensified in the presence of colleagues like Pollock but was eased by music. She bought a recording of Schubert's *Unfinished Symphony* and enjoyed a picnic of claret and macaroons outside on the lawn of the Esplanade while attending a Boston Pops concert alone. She also enjoyed the companionship of Stanley Boggs, a friend nine years her junior who had also been at Copán:

He likes practically everyone and is not taken in by many. He accepts life casually, is not over ambitious but sincerely interested and serious in his work. . . . A remark of his that I have ever been grateful for is when he called Gus a "natural born gentleman." I like, too, his casual acceptance of our acquaintance, which to me is a joy since our discrepancy in ages prevents my thinking of him sentimentally . . . which in my restless and lonely present state I could fall into very easily with a more eligible man. Harry could probably disturb me more . . . but I don't want any complexities within the Institution."[30]

Although she did not wish it, "complexities" did eventually develop for Tania.

Adding to her restlessness, her mother wrote that Peggy and Linton Satterthwaite had separated. In her diary, Tania confided, "I can't help wondering what has happened . . . and feel a little guiltily that I should have reacted differently to this two years ago. I should like to see him, though, but I am not sure that he would care to tell me."[31] This is the only indication in her diaries that her feelings for Satterthwaite had at one time been deeper than friendship, an idea that her sister, Kay, passed on to her children years later. In a letter to Satterthwaite, Tania wrote, "Since I saw you last, I have been rather ashamed that I was slow to realize what difficult times you have been going through. I do hope your problems will find a happy solution and wish you all possible luck."[32]

In time the Satterthwaites reconciled, and their devotion remained strong the rest of their lives.

Tania grappled with other large issues, coming to terms with her political views and philosophy. She became engrossed in a collection of philosophical essays titled *I Believe*. In her diary, she listed the contributing writers, among them Havelock Ellis, Stuart Chase, and Franz Boas, along with the key points of each essay. She then noted her criticism or approval of each.[33] Of Ellen Glasgow's essay, she wrote that it was "very confused," then quoted, "The greatest need of the modern world is not for a multitude of machines but for a new and a higher conception of God."[34] To this Tania added, "Me too." This calls into question Michael Coe's assertion in *Breaking the Maya Code* that Tania was an atheist. It suggests rather that she may have expressed such ideas simply to stimulate lively discussion with Coe.[35] If so, it is but one example of Tania's "contrariness" mentioned by many of her friends and colleagues.

The political atmosphere in Cambridge in 1940 was decidedly supportive of the British effort to defeat Germany. However, Tania forced herself to look deeper at the issues "amid the conflicting waves of propaganda and counter-propaganda."[36] Having ties on both sides, she felt drawn to the Quakers and their international relief efforts.[37] She was greatly concerned about measures to restrict the freedom of speech of organizations in the United States with Communist or Nazi ties. She wrote, "Non-democratic moves to preserve democracy seem rather incongruous since we were always taught to believe that freedom of expression of opinion and of organization is essential to the preservation of a democratic state." And later: "Of course, a modification of democracy is preferable to its destruction and I suppose I must countenance if not approve it."[38]

Tania now resumed work on a fountain design for the village of Copán.[39] She also excitedly noted in her diary, "I have 'discovered' the Dresden Codex and am playing with it in odd moments."[40] Her interest in the Codex remained strong throughout that fall and winter. She also worked with the hieroglyphic inscriptions on Stelae 1 and 3 of Piedras Negras, fretting that she never had enough time to spend on them.[41] It is evident that the inscriptions at this site continued to intrigue Tania over the years. Her first published article, "An Inscription on a Jade Probably Carved at Piedras Negras," appeared in 1944. Sixteen years later, Tania wrote her breakthrough *American Antiquity* article that was based on the inscriptions of this site, changing the direction of Maya research.

In February 1941 Tania received word from her parents that they would be moving to Burlington, Iowa. The chemical firm of Day and Zimmermann had been commissioned by the U.S. government and had hired her father as chief chemist for an ordnance plant he was to help design and set up. Tania was glad that Avenir would have challenging work, but she also worried that the move would be a strain for him: "Skipper's failing health I have to accept I suppose, but his depressed state of mind constantly worries me. He has such a joyful interest in living sometimes, and I don't like to see him turn away from it as if he were merely dreading and waiting for the end."[42]

Helping to sort through the contents of their home was a somber, introspective task for Tania: "It is so hard to part with old mementos, but now that it is finished it isn't really the loss that I regret but that there was after all so little to lose, that that life, happy as it was, produced so little and contained such meager experiences."[43] Of the family mementos, she selected only two boxes of books and several photographs from Russia.

Returning to Cambridge, she continued to examine her political beliefs. She wrote, "I can't see my way clear to identifying myself with any general movement."[44] Tania began to attend Quaker meetings, where she heard members of a relief team who had recently returned from Europe report on tremendous food shortages throughout the continent. She participated in discussions about Mahatma Gandhi, a man she greatly admired for leading the passive resistance movement in India. However, in her diary she confided, "I feel my vices and follies too strongly in the presence of Quakers. But that worst fault, getting too excited about political questions and prejudices, bothers me most of all."[45]

Through attending the Quaker meetings, Tania began to connect with people around her. However, she felt isolated at the Carnegie office, where tension over the war was building: "For the first time in my life I'm in a situation where I find it difficult to make friends. I seem to be almost antagonistic to people here, even those I like. There are so few points of contact."[46] When Kidder's wife organized a group of women at the museum to knit sweaters to send to Europe, she did not solicit Tania's help. Overly sensitive, Tania interpreted this as a snub and in her diary wondered, "I am not liked there I know, but why?"[47]

Tania had recently read Pearl S. Buck's latest book, *Of Men and Women*, in an attempt to understand why certain married women seemed hostile to her. One day on her way home from a tennis lesson, Tania ran into a woman who noticed she was carrying Buck's book. She later noted, "I could almost see her bristle and get very polite. . . . I'm not sure I can quite understand why married women . . . are so anxious to assert their superiority over women who are single. . . . [T]hey seem to see in marriage a certain duty a woman is neglecting if she remains single."[48]

Her social sphere included many married couples, but the Shooks were the closest. It was at one of their frequent dinner parties that Tania confronted another problem as a single woman. A young couple was also invited for dinner, and when the wife went to the kitchen to help, Tania remained in the living room with the two men. Ignoring her, the young man spoke directly to Shook about the cost of living and the importance of purchasing real estate. When Shook left the room to fix more drinks, the man apologized for talking so long about such matters. Tania pointed out that these things were important to her as well. Describing this encounter, she wrote, "He remarked, 'But most women don't worry about such things!' I felt like saying, 'No, of course not. Let's talk about dresses or Clark Gable,' but refrained. I haven't the art of doing it inoffensively."[49]

Tania's frustrations came to a head in July while preparing to visit her parents in Iowa: "I'm about fed up with Cambridge, 10 Frisbie and my own inertia. . . . Pen and ink line drawings and my wobbly hand and the fact that I accomplish nothing in particular is certainly getting me down and making me at times very irritable." Later she added, "It will be so nice to sleep in a house, to have friends to talk to, but most of all I want to change myself. I am disgusted with my own feelings of failure, particularly with vague feelings of unfounded resentment, against automobiles, against fashions, against people, and against words like 'democracy,' 'Germany,' 'Nazism' and against bombs."[50] In Iowa she attended lavish parties given by her parents' friends and colleagues and saw her father's laboratory. After a rejuvenating visit, she went to the family cabin in New Hampshire for a quiet week alone. The trip proved to be a balm for her spirits, and she returned to Cambridge in a more positive mood.

The mood was short-lived. By mid-October Tania's father was admitted to the hospital with phlebitis. In her diary, she worried that Avenir was "evidently not yet well" and added, "[H]is illness has sombered everything."[51] Her despair intensified with news of the devastating Japanese air attack on American forces in Pearl Harbor on December 7. She wrote, "Since we are in the conflict, there is no course but to fight hard and only privately to keep a balanced sense of tolerance and regret for the whole business. 1941 . . . will be the year of the Greater World War."[52]

Throughout World War II, Tania tried to find a balance between her patriotism and her abhorrence of war. In January she wondered, "Will nations . . . ever merge into humanity? I think they must, for some unfortunates like me have already widened our allegiance and scattered it over the globe. But we are living somewhat out of our time."[53] Later that winter, she wrote, "Every Thursday, I listen to the 'American Forum of the Air' and each time I want to ask that same unanswerable question. How can I kill my 'brother'? How can I divert my loyalty to the human race for loyalty to a part which is less than the whole? . . . Does the paradox of good coming from evil not sow any seeds of doubt?"[54]

Tania felt isolated in her views from most of the people around her and so tended to stay quietly to herself. Insecure about her temporary position with the CIW, she wrote, "I had always thought Harvard would offer plenty of opportunity for interesting acquaintances and am disappointed to find myself stranded and quite alone. . . . I have decided that if my status with the Institution is still 'temporary,' it will be the end of it this year."[55] Another year would pass before she became an official member of the Carnegie staff. She learned of her appointment in a roundabout manner when Kidder told her she needed to sign up for their group life insurance plan. Answering that she did not qualify for the plan because she was not on the staff, Kidder was surprised and saw to it that she received official notification.[56] In April 1943 she wrote simply, "George [Brainerd] and Karl [Ruppert], still waiting for their war jobs, have combined to keep me busy at the office. I hardly think I can bear it when they go, though I am an institution member now and am hoping for approval of my publication."[57]

Many at the CIW had found ways to become involved in the war effort, adding to Tania's sense of isolation in Cambridge.[58] Shook moved his family to Guatemala and remained there during the war years. As an archaeologist, he and others, such as Ledyard Smith and Ruppert, had an excellent cover for doing FBI intelligence work. Shook later served as the director of a vast quinine-producing operation, vital for treatment of malaria among Allied troops in the Pacific.[59] Pollock was commissioned as captain in the U.S. Army Air Corps and served in Europe from 1942 to 1945, when he was discharged with the rank of major.[60] Ruppert briefly worked in intelligence before signing on with the Red Cross as an ambulance driver in Burma and Italy.[61] Tania wrote, "It's so awfully lonely here. . . . [A]ll the office force is absent. . . . I don't suppose [Bill] Andrews and [George] Brainerd will stay long after their return."[62] She was correct. In 1942 Andrews joined the OSS in Italy. Tania noted that Boggs too seemed "to be in something hushed,"[63] while Longyear had begun working on experimental magnetrons for radar at the Radiation Laboratory at MIT.

However, it was Strömsvik's departure that most affected Tania. He joined the Norwegian navy and, refusing an officer's commission, served as a sailor on a destroyer on convoy duty in the North Atlantic. He was transferred to a base in England and participated in the invasion of Normandy, for which he was eventually decorated.[64] En route to Halifax to report for duty onboard ship, Strömsvik stopped in Boston and shared a sentimental dinner with Tania: "We ate steamed clams in a little restaurant in Boston, drank several martinis and then I saw him off on his train and came home and bawled, I don't know just why. Maybe because his life has completed such a tragic circle and maybe because it is only in such an incongruous person that I can find a close community of attitude."[65]

In fall 1942 Tania found her own way to make a contribution to the war effort by enrolling in a ship-drafting course in Boston.[66] She was able to attend only a few classes, for it was at this time that she received the devastating news of her father's death in Iowa. She wrote,

> For the last few days I have only been aware how remote and irrelevant are our emotions from our understanding of reality. Some sort of strange illusions seem to cause our tears and laughing while the world that we know with all its changes and events goes on coldly, impersonally. Mother's strained serious face when I met her at the station[,] . . . the news that Skipper died and the plain ridiculous fact that I don't believe it. If I've ever loved anyone, it has been Skipper. I relied on his judgment, he bolstered my ego by his unselfish love for me and offered me protection from being hurt by the indifference of others, and gave me a philosophy of life and a certain standard that I accepted because it was his.[67]

Her loss was profound. No one filled the void left by her father's death, though Tania gradually came to rely on the advice and inspiration of other men such as Morley, Kidder, and Alfred Tozzer.

In her grief she found solace in music and art and, as always, in books. Her friend Helen Hale had a piano in her apartment, which she made available for Tania's use. At Briggs and Briggs, a music store in Harvard Square, she bought copies of the Brahms and Chopin *Waltzes* and began to brush up on her rusty skills. She found, to her surprise, that although her fingers were stiff, the music came back to her quickly.[68] She also continued to attend concerts by the Boston Symphony, and after one she wrote, "The music was excellent. Something about its beauty of expression that is incontrovertibly right. It is order in a chaotic world and meaning in a senseless life."[69]

Tania found support in her meetings with Morley: "Dr. Morley is my one source of encouragement. . . . He is receptive to my views, but what a task to follow his agile mind! I can barely keep up and feel exhausted at the end of the day."[70] She also enjoyed once again the companionship of Shepard, who was in Cambridge to confer with Kidder: "We have had amazing discussions, however frictions here and there are very apparent. . . . Most everybody except Kidder and Brew seem to disapprove of Anna. Her intense concentration on her work and insistence on thoroughness and accuracy seems to irritate a lot of people."[71] The two women continued their stimulating discussions on art and aesthetics in letters that spanned the next two decades.

Tania's reading also reflected this interest:

I am preoccupied with a book on Modern Art by Cheney and neglecting my work. It seems to me that I never fully realized before the aims of modern painting. . . . The emphasis of modern art on pure abstraction, like the reliance of scientific fields on pure mathematics, opens infinite possibilities for progress. . . . Whenever I have tried to sketch I have been puzzled to know what to draw of the innumerable things that one could see and of the sometimes conflicting qualities of the same thing. Often shadows appear at once blue and gray and mauve in rapid succession. Often I have been quickly bored with rendering some complex pattern or texture and have ignored it merely because it was wearisome to do. It never occurred to me to paint only what I wanted to paint by deliberate choice.[72]

At the office Tania was finalizing the text for *An Album of Maya Architecture*. Margaret Harrison, editor of Carnegie Institution publications, described the status of Tania's project: "The volume, to be ready for publication by the end of 1943, will contain a short introduction and 34 mechanically plotted perspective drawings rendered in black-and-white wash. Each plate is accompanied by a descriptive comment and a pen-and-ink sketch showing the degree of certainty in the restoration."[73]

In a letter to Mason, Tania revealed that she was struggling with writing the book's introduction and commentary: "I want to tell you how much I admire your *Middle America Handbook*. . . . I do envy the facility and grace of your expression, especially when I tackle the text of my book and discover myself virtually illiterate."[74] The preparation for her book would drag on for another full year, by which time she confided in her diary, "[M]y mind is like a soggy sponge just as I must finish my manuscript. I wound it up with a flossy blurb about the aspirations of mankind, and there it is."[75] Kidder did not share her pessimism. He wrote, "Miss T. Proskouriakoff's album of restored drawings of Maya temples and groups of buildings is now in press. It is believed that in addition to its value to Middle Americanists, this work will be of much interest to students of Old World archaeology and to architects."[76]

According to Shook, it was the publication of the *Album*, first envisioned by Morley in 1938, that "finally put Tania on the map" in Mesoamerican archaeology.[77] Even as she was writing the final drafts for this book, she was starting work on another, for which she was particularly well suited. This new project would involve a return to Central America but this time into entirely new territories.

CHAPTER SEVEN

Reconnaissance Trips through Central America (1944–1947)

In 1944, with many of the Carnegie archaeologists still involved in the war effort, Kidder felt increasingly concerned that his budget for the Division of Historical Research would be cut drastically. He approached Tania with the idea of taking an extended trip to survey the major archaeological sites of Central America. He thought she should visit as many sites as possible, not scrimping on her expenses.[1] This was unusual, as strict accounting procedures had always been required of Carnegie archaeologists, who were expected to limit their personal travel expenses. As Shook explained, "We had to be quite frugal. Nothing was written down by way of regulations, but there was simply a tradition. Your food, transportation and lodging all had to be covered by $5.00 a day."[2]

With work completed on her *Album*, Tania had already begun a new project involving the detailed analysis of Maya sculpture bearing dates that could be correlated to our calendar. As Kidder described in his *Year Book* report, Tania intended to find "reliable stylistic criteria . . . for the dating of the many monuments which bear either no dates or illegible ones."[3] As Tania enjoyed telling later in her life, the impetus for this project was a friendly debate with Morley over a date he had attributed to a particular stela. She disagreed with his conclusion and began working on a system of graphs that she believed would more reliably place undated monuments in their appropriate period.[4] The opportunity offered by Kidder to get an overview of the region fit well with Tania's project, and she immediately began preparations for the trip.

When she went to get the shots needed for travel in the tropics, she found that the doctor knew "nothing whatever about typhoid immunization [and] had never heard of sero-bactezine or oral vaccine."[5] She received a series of typhoid shots that caused her to stay in bed for several days. Later she chided herself, "It may be malingering, for I want to read the latest Perry Mason."[6] Her lifelong passion for mysteries and detective stories, well known among her friends, grew more intense in the war years.[7]

During her preparations, she learned of major political upheavals in Central America: "There is revolution in Guatemala, Salvador and Honduras. It looks bad for my trip."[8] Continued instability prevented her from traveling to El Salvador and Honduras; however, her trip to Guatemala went as planned when, in the aftermath of the revolution of October 20, 1944, officials successfully held free elections.[9]

Before leaving, Tania spent the holidays with her mother in Philadelphia. In 1943, less than a year after her husband's death in Iowa, Alla had returned east, leaving her job as women's medical examiner at the ordnance plant that Avenir had helped to set up. In the hope that her mother would move to Cambridge, Tania tried repeatedly to get the Massachusetts State Medical Board to consider her medical credentials. Although Tania submitted a copy of Alla's diploma, the requests were denied. Conditions in Russia prevented direct communication with the university in Tomsk, which could have verified her attendance, and so, in spite of Tania's efforts, Alla returned to Philadelphia.[10]

On New Year's Day, Tania returned alone to Boston by train. Indulging in a favorite pastime while traveling, she observed her fellow passengers. She later described them in her diary: "Girls were offering seats to hefty sailors and a very drunk flossie was wrestling with a helpless officer, who . . . was describing his wedding on leave as 'very gay.'"[11] The mood on the train to Boston was almost giddy, reflecting the dramatic shift in the war. The year's bombing campaign over England by the Luftwaffe had failed to break the English spirit, and Allied forces were now on the offensive in Europe. German oil reserves were drastically depleted, and Russian troops were within sixty kilometers of Berlin.

At the office, Kidder told Tania he had decided to accompany her on part of her trip, eliminating the need for introductions. In a letter to Satterthwaite, she wrote, "[Kidder] conceived the idea that he and Kirk Bryan [Harvard professor of geology][12] and I might go to Mexico together. Plans with A.V.K. [Kidder] are generally fluid, and if it doesn't work out, I'll try to get a letter from him to [Alfonso] Caso when we meet in Guatemala. In any case, I do appreciate your introductions for I'd like to call on as many colleagues of ours as I can in Mexico."[13]

Tania spent the remaining weeks in January making a will and renewing her passport.[14] The problem with her passport was reminiscent of an earlier one Tania had shortly after moving to Massachusetts. Her diary entry from that year reads, "Yesterday I tried to register as a voter but was not permitted to without Skipper's naturalization papers. I decided to get my own and went to the Naturalization Bureau. . . . [R]ed tape and nonsense, silly questions on dotted lines, and a marriage certificate of my parents was requested[,] . . . everything sublime buried in the ridiculous. . . . Fiction sometimes is more real than life under a bureaucracy."[15]

Tania was finally ready to leave, and on January 29 she reached New Orleans. From there she caught the midnight plane and arrived in Guatemala City early the next morning. The city, founded in 1776 after an earthquake destroyed the colonial capital at Antigua, is located in a valley surrounded by volcanic mountains. Once one of the finest cities in Central America, Guatemala City is renowned for its beautiful colonial architecture. From the air, the approach over the mountains is dramatic.[16] In a letter to her sister, Kay, she described the flight: "[N]othing but clouds beneath us to the horizon—it was thrilling and a little frightening. Our plane was half an hour late and I had visions of it diving at random through that unbroken sea and hitting a mountain. However we suddenly passed the clouds—and there were peaks and volcanoes and gorges all around us—you can't imagine the scenery—it is terrific!"[17] For Tania, who preferred other modes of travel, it was a tiring experience.

She went directly to her room at the Pensión Guerault, which she described in the same letter to Kay:

> One enters a tiled patio with bedrooms all around. In the middle is a jungle of potted plants so thick that one can't get through though there are steps leading down. All around the jungle are bird cages, so that one is awakened each morning with twittering and song. The room I have is huge. . . . [T]he bed, of course is hard as rock and comes up in the middle, but the bathtubs are eight feet long and the meals are super. . . . I hate to leave this place for the miserable beans and tortillas we are likely to get on the road.

After settling into her room, the first detail Tania attended to was obtaining the proper papers from Guatemalan officials for traveling to and working at sites throughout the country. This accomplished, she joined Kidder for a drive to inspect the ruins of Kaminaljuyu.[18] Although today much of the surrounding area has been bulldozed for suburban development, in the 1940s the site was still green pastureland on the western edge of the capital. In 1935, when officials of a local school wanted to expand their soccer field, several of the two hundred mounds of this ancient city were dug up, exposing stone walls, plaster floors, and whole pottery vessels. The minister of public education contacted the Carnegie office, and together they determined that a brief excavation should be conducted. Once the complexity of the layers of structures and tombs was understood, a larger project was begun, led first by Oliver G. Ricketson and later, Kidder. Over the years the project unearthed many burials, including tombs of extraordinary historical significance.[19] Tania was fascinated with what she saw during her first visit: "The size and number of mounds is impressive."[20] However, years would pass before she became directly involved with the work there.

Tania began arranging the details for the next leg of her trip. En route to Mexico she would visit Finca Porvenir, the quinine farm that Shook was supervising on the western border of Guatemala. Tania was to travel with Ledyard Smith, one of the Carnegie archaeologists she first met in 1937 at Piedras Negras. The two had become friends working at the Carnegie office in Cambridge, where he had often joined Tania and the lunch club. This marked the start of a warm friendship that endured many years under difficult situations and stressful field conditions.

Augustus Ledyard Smith was born in 1901 into a prominent Wisconsin family. The son of Mary Eliot and Franklin Taylor Smith III, he attended boarding schools in Ouchy, Switzerland, and Concord, New Hampshire, with his older brother, Robert.[21] He received his degree from Harvard University in 1925. He went to work in his family's business, but in 1927 Ricketson, a fellow member of the Fly Club, asked him to join the Carnegie excavation he was directing at Uaxactún. Restless and eager for adventure, Smith signed on, thus beginning a long, productive career in Maya archaeology.

Located north of Tikal in the rugged Petén region of Guatemala, Uaxactún has yielded much valuable information on the Maya civilization.[22] In 1934 Smith took over responsibilities as director of the project, which now included Shook and Pollock, another Fly Club member. The men formed a strong bond and, along with Tania and others of the Carnegie Division of Historical Research, worked closely together at the site of Mayapán late in their careers.

During the war years, Smith and his first wife had divorced. The secrecy required by his intelligence work for the FBI contributed to the breakup, a detail he revealed to his son only many years later.[23] Smith next began a survey of sites in highland Guatemala. This involved "archaeological reconnaissance in the departments of Huehuetenango and El Quiche to obtain as much information as possible . . . as to both hilltop and valley sites with a view to selecting representative examples of each type for future excavation."[24] It was this project that would eventually include Tania.

Less than a week after arriving in Guatemala City, Tania was prepared to join Smith and César Tejeda for the trip in the CIW's station wagon. The younger brother of the artist Antonio Tejeda, César had made a reputation "for his ability in mending and restoring pottery . . . and showed outstanding promise as an archaeologist"[25] while working at Kaminaljuyu in 1942. He attended the Escuela Nacional de Antropología in Mexico City with support from the Rockefeller Foundation and had since worked closely with Smith on his survey. Together they drove first to the town of Santa Lucía Cotzumalguapa, where they took rooms at a pensión in order to visit Finca El Baúl, a coffee plantation. El Baúl had in its garden a "collection of sculptured heads[,] . . . pieces familiar from the Thompson report,"[26] which Tania wanted to look over.

They drove the next day to Lake Atitlán where they met with Kidder, Bryan, and Robert Smith. More conservative than his younger brother, Robert Smith had joined the work at Uaxactún several years after Ledyard. As a member of the Carnegie, he made his home in Guatemala City with his wife, Becky.[27] The group met to talk, then hired a launch to take them across the lake to the village of Santiago Atitlán.

Eleanor Lothrop, wife of the Harvard archaeologist Sam Lothrop, described the area in her 1948 book, *Throw Me a Bone*: "Lake Atitlán is a storybook lake. The water is deep blue, shot with occasional green, and an unbroken chain of mountains encircles it. Huge volcanoes tower in the background, purple and brown cones with cottony clouds covering their tips. . . . Santiago Atitlán is the most colorful, the most charming . . . place I've ever lived."[28]

After the trip across the lake, Kidder and the others gathered for a beer at a bar overhanging the water. In his diary, Kidder wrote, "[I] tried to show off the swarming of the fish for Tania, but none rose to my bit of bread." He earlier had described the day as being "of sky so blue that Tania, who did a watercolor sketch[,] . . . said there was no paint in her box that could come even near it." Kidder enjoyed her company and described an evening when he invited her to his room: "leaving the door open, *pour les convenances*," they talked "until 10."[29] The affection was mutual and meant even more to Tania since the death of her father.

Smith and Tania traveled on to Finca Porvenir where they spent several days in meetings. Shook's wife was here at this time, and Tania was happy to see her. The meetings left little time for the two friends, and Ginny later wrote to Tania, "What disappointed me a great deal was not to see more of you. . . . [T]here were so many things I wanted to ask you. . . . [N]ext time can't you arrange to do something in Guatemala instead of popping off practically immediately to Mexico? . . . Ed said you did some very nice water colors while you were up here. How I would like to see them. Please do one of Tajamulco, it is my favorite volcano."

Shook concluded the joint letter, "Your few days in Porvenir were a great stimulant and I got much pleasure from all the discussions."[30]

Shook accompanied Smith and Tania across the border into Mexico. They had planned to visit the ruins at Izapa on the Pacific coastal plain of southern Chiapas, but the paperwork at the border took so long that they had to drive directly to the town of Tapachula. The two men only had time to be sure Tania was settled into a hotel before they headed back to Guatemala. Tania wrote, "The town looks very down at the heels, but my plane leaves tomorrow at 6:30 A.M. so I shall not spend much time here at the Gran Hotel Internacional, which is . . . anything but grand."[31] The next day she flew over the hills of Chiapas and the high mountains beyond Ixtepec to Oaxaca.

Although there is evidence that the Valley of Oaxaca has been populated for ten thousand years, the city of Oaxaca de Juárez was founded by Spanish settlers shortly after Francisco Orozco conquered a hilltop fort in 1521. By decree from the Spanish crown, the city was built to conform to other colonial cities of the era, with a cathedral, a central plaza, and stone streets laid out in an orderly grid.[32] Oaxaca has a calming effect on the visitor, with elegant wrought-iron balconies and soft splashes of paint on the stucco walls of the buildings. Tania spent four days here with trips to the nearby mountaintop ruins of Monte Albán, where restoration work was under way. She wrote, "As I reached the main group, Mr. Acosta who is in charge very kindly guided me around and explained the progress of the work."[33] She drew a site plan and later at the museum made sketches of pieces in its sculpture collection. One day she hired a car to drive fifty kilometers east to visit the ruins of Mitla, known for its distinctive murals and mosaic-decorated palaces.

Train service between Oaxaca and Mexico City had been disrupted for the past five months, and plane reservations were not available for another week, so Tania decided to travel by bus. The overland trip north to the elaborate baroque colonial city of Puebla took twelve hours, during which she noted "the very beautiful coloring of rock and vegetation."[34] In Puebla she hired a car to drive to Cholula, the sacred city founded along an ancient trade route. Site of the largest-known pyramid in the New World, Cholula "had a reputation as a center for trade in luxury items such as jewels, precious stones, and fine featherwork."[35] In a letter to Shook, she wrote, "I am certainly grateful to you for suggesting that I go to Puebla on my way to Mexico. . . . Cholula was certainly worth seeing. They are building a new museum there and have models of the pyramid . . . and the museum at Puebla has quite a lot of sculpture."[36]

Tania then continued on to Mexico City, using this as her base to travel to sites such as Teotihuacán and Xochicalco. With letters of introduction from Satterthwaite, Kidder, and Shook, she met many people active in Mexican archaeology. Perhaps the best known of these was Alfonso Caso, who was director of the ongoing project at Monte Albán. While visiting the Museo Nacional, Tania spent hours with Caso, who told her about an exciting new discovery at the site. Shook suggested that she should contact Bodil Christensen, a Danish anthropologist who studied papermaking and witchcraft in remote villages in central Mexico.[37] Bodil accompanied Tania on a trip to Veracruz to survey the ruins of El Tajín, an important center that had thrived between A.D. 300 and 1100, when the site was located on an east-west trade route.

Tania and Bodil traveled by bus through lush countryside toward the Gulf coastal plain. They crossed the dramatic Sierra Madre Oriental along the way. Arriving in Papantla, they were met by friends of Bodil who ran a lucrative vanilla bean business and who put them up in luxurious rooms in their home. They also arranged for horses for the thirteen-kilometer ride to the ruins. Tania spent the day exploring and later wrote to Shook, "Tajín left me practically breathless. I never imagined it as such a tremendous site. Except for glyphs, it has everything that the Maya have plus the darndest roof construction I've ever seen. . . . Most of it is still under bush, and not much that has not been excavated can be seen, but the size and number of pyramids is really impressive."[38] Excavations at El Tajín since her visit have revealed glyphs that list the names of warriors who took prisoners.

Two days later the women returned to Mexico City. In the next weeks Tania visited many more sites, including Tula, Teotihuacán, and Malinalco. Although she came down with bronchitis, she was greatly stimulated by her time in Mexico. She wrote to Shook, "I met Marquina and

Tania at El Tajín, Veracruz, Mexico, undated. Courtesy of Mike Beetem.

Caso, both of whom, I think, are perfectly charming. . . . There is a wonderful exhibit of masks at the Modern Art Institute . . . and they have published an excellently illustrated catalogue."[39] This exhibition had been put together by Miguel Covarrubias and used new dramatic techniques for display, which appealed to Tania's aesthetic sensibility.[40]

She continued in her letter to Shook, "Mexico is jam full of people, deputies for the Pan American Congress and tourists, and it seems to have grown up tremendously since I was here last." The congress Tania referred to was the Inter-American Conference on the Problems of War and Peace that was held from February 21 to March 8 and attended by delegates from every North and South American nation except Argentina. It resulted in the signing of the Act of Chapultepec, a pact of mutual defense for aggression against any of the signatory countries.[41] Mexico City was bustling with delegations, and Tania was energized. She concluded her letter to Shook, "I'm having an awfully good time and picking up Spanish fast, talking to people on busses[,] . . . but if I get nothing else out of this trip it has certainly boosted my interest in archaeology." She was impressed by the amount of ongoing archaeological work, and her affection for the people and places she encountered was genuine. In the years to come, Tania often returned to Mexico City, finding there inspiration, friendship, and a renewed sense of direction.

Back in Cambridge, Tania initially felt energized for resuming her work. However, soon after her arrival, the news of President Roosevelt's death from a massive cerebral hemorrhage left Tania deeply saddened and introspective. In her diary, she wrote, "Even though I personally disagree with much in Roosevelt's foreign policy . . . he was a gallant figure and he was wise, or at least clever. We haven't another who can command the respect which he commanded abroad. . . . [W]e've really lost someone."[42]

Other than this passage about Roosevelt, during the time Tania wrote little in her diary of world events, though they were decidedly dramatic. On May 8 Germany formally surrendered. Ruppert and Pollock returned from Italy, and both stopped by the office. Tania wrote pensively in her diary, "I had a talk with Karl. . . . [H]e is going back to the war in the Pacific I am sure. There is nothing for him here and he mentioned his disappointment at 'coming home.' It is frightful to think that it takes a war to give a man the opportunity for service for which he longs! He is happier being of use in that horror and misery than being neglected here."[43] Of the successful testing of the first atomic bomb at Alamogordo, New Mexico, and the surrender of Japan, she made no diary entries, although she certainly was aware of their global significance.

Concerned that the inspiration from her travels was waning, she tried to complete the watercolor of the volcano she had promised the Shooks. Frustrated with her efforts, she wrote to them, "I don't think it's much use to try unless you can send me another photo taken from your front porch. . . . When I try to use my imagination it looks like Pennsylvania no matter how many palms and bananas I put in. It's not an excuse for poor composition and inadequate technique, but a photo of the place might at least remind me of it."[44]

Throughout 1946 Tania developed her method of dating stelae through graphs of stylistic elements that would result in her next book. That winter she wrote, "Harry tells me to keep on with my graph making, though his attitude seems skeptical. I am not too sure myself."[45] She read books on art, such as *The Aesthetic Adventure* by William Gaunt, and continued her lively conversations with Shepard when she was in town. These discussions carried over into their correspondence. Shepard wrote to Tania, "My trip east was tantalizingly brief . . . but I'm glad to have had an opportunity to learn more about your style study. I sincerely hope you have recovered from your discouragement regarding your method because your approach is thoroughly sound and your procedure well thought out. . . . I'm so sick of all the brandishing about of 'brilliant' intuitions innocent of any test that it is heartening to know your study is being made in the particular way that it is."[46] Along with this encouragement, she included suggestions of books and articles she had found helpful in her research into symmetry and psychological studies of art.

In 1943 Kidder had released Tania from much of the drafting work she had been doing for others so that she could pursue her own projects,[47] however she accepted Tozzer's request to draw the gold discs from the Sacred Cenote at Chichén Itzá. She wrote, "They are magnificent, worked in repoussé with figures and scroll work. . . . I will probably be very foolish to take it on, but don't know who else could do them. . . . [A] pencil drawing of mine might be better than what they would otherwise do."[48] This would not be the only time Tania would deal with artifacts dredged from the Sacred Cenote, as this material took up considerable time, talent, and energy in her later years.

During this period, Tania also renewed an old interest in India. She read the Upanishads, ancient Sanskrit texts from the eighth century B.C. In her diary, she quoted, "Who knoweth all things are Self; for him what grief existeth, what delusion, when he gazeth on the oneness. . . . Aye, who so seeth all things in that self and Self in everything; from that he'll no more hide." Commenting on the difficulty of translating these ancient manuscripts, she wrote, "[W]e have no words of comparable connotation. A concept embodied in a word is a large accretion of experiences and opinions. . . . How different must have been in an older civilization the concept of 'organism' which occurs in a translation of the Upanishads. Even a man is a different creature when he is related to gods than when he is descended from apes. The amazing thing is that ancient books do at times strike a sympathetic note."[49]

Tania was also reading a book by Nehru. She noted that India's quest for independence from England was justified but that Gandhi's legacy "will not be the liberation of India but the effect of his thought on coming generations." Questioning Nehru's assessment that population growth had little impact on his country, she wrote, "I cannot share his views. I think it is the greatest dilemma that faces us and that peace is a dream without population control."[50]

At work, Tania's associates in the Division of Historical Research were facing a dilemma of another sort. The CIW was now under new leadership. Succeeding John C. Merriam as president was Vannevar Bush, a physicist who had worked on developing MIT's first computer and later on the Manhattan Project.[51] His priorities for the CIW lay with the physical sciences. Kidder found he had to argue for funds to continue the division's archaeological investigations in Central America. As early as 1945 Tania described in her diary a dinner with Ruppert when she had "spilled the story of the division's plight of which he apparently knew nothing," adding that they had "gloomed about it together."[52] In September 1946 all available division archaeologists were requested to attend a conference during which they attempted to formulate a joint program they hoped Bush would consider worthy of funding. Late in life Tania related, "[Bush] would have liked us to ask for a lot of money for equipment, and gadgets. . . . He was interested in astronomy, in money for enormous telescopes. . . . If we had asked for magnometers to find remains under the earth . . . he might have kept us on."[53] In 1946 she wrote, "It seems to me we failed pretty successfully . . . and let A.V.K. down. . . . The end of the conference was pretty grim."[54] Although the tension and uncertainties Kidder had been dealing with were now out in the open, more speculation and debate would occur in the years ahead before the fate of the Division of Historical Research and its associates was determined.

At this disturbing time for the future of Mesoamerican archaeology, word reached Cambridge about a startling new discovery in Central America. Giles Healey, an American photographer and explorer, had traveled to the remote eastern rainforest of Chiapas to make a film on the primitive Lacandon Indians for the American Fruit Company. While there, several Lacandons guided him to the previously unrecorded site of Bonampak. In his report for the *Carnegie Institution Year Book*, Kidder described the vivid murals Healey found on the walls in one of the structures as "indeed the single most important discovery ever made in the Maya field."[55] It took many years for the significance of these murals to be more widely recognized. In 1995 Yale University scholar, Mary Ellen Miller, wrote in *National Geographic Magazine*, "Mayanists had long believed that Classic Maya civilization, spanning A.D. 250 to 900, was a peaceful Eden ruled by benevolent astronomer-priests. Yet Bonampak's graphic depiction of combat . . . demonstrates that the Maya exhibited all the flaws and grace of humanity."[56]

When photographs of the discovery arrived at the Carnegie offices, Tania excitedly mentioned them in her diary: "Healey sends a photo of another beautiful lintel . . . and Tejeda reports that there are enough murals there to keep him busy three to six months!"[57] Kidder began planning a joint Carnegie–University of Pennsylvania expedition to view the murals firsthand. He suggested that Tania accompany the group at the end of her scheduled field season in Guatemala with Smith, but she wrote, "I'm afraid it will be a tough trip on top of the Highlands."[58] The expedition, headed by Ruppert, included J. Eric S. Thompson, Strömsvik, Tejeda, Healey, and Agustín Villagra, an artist with the Mexican Instituto Nacional de Antropología e Historia.[59] Although Tania later coauthored the Carnegie publication on Bonampak with Ruppert, she never visited the site.

In January 1947 Alla accompanied Tania to Central America. They met in Philadelphia, then took the train to New Orleans, with a brief stopover in Washington, D.C., where they visited the National Gallery. Describing a tea with old Russian friends, Tania noted "[They] seem very remote to me now[,] . . . remnants of another and different era. . . . It is difficult to find a point of contact."[60] In New Orleans Tania and her mother stayed overnight at the Roosevelt Hotel. The next day they shopped, then dined at Antoine's before catching the night flight to Yucatán.

In Mérida Tania spent some time with Morley, who was now sixty-four years old. He and his wife lived during the winter months at Chenkú, a house they had renovated on a former henequen plantation just outside Mérida. His book, *The Ancient Maya*, had been published the year before and was now in its second printing. He was working on a dictionary of Maya hieroglyphs and writing guidebooks to be used at Chichén Itzá and Uxmal. Tania wrote, "Went with Morley to Uxmal. We talked ourselves hoarse and had a lunch of tamales and oranges. . . . Morley still goes stela hunting and they have just found a few fragments of glyphs on the platform in front of the Governor's Palace."[61]

The next day Tania and Alla flew to Guatemala City. After taking a room at the Pensión Guerault, Tania got in touch with Carnegie colleagues who were in the city. They were invited to tea at Barbara Kidder's and were met back at the pension by Ginny Shook, who asked them to come to their home for lunch. Robert Smith stopped by to pick up the two women so they could see the new anthropological museum he had been working on with a group of influential Guatemalans. Tania wrote, "[The museum] is very impressive, and he has done a splendid job on it."[62] This was the Museo Nacional de Arqueología y Etnología, which now houses the world's largest collection of Maya sculpture from Guatemala and displays an original reconstruction drawing of Uaxactún by Tania.[63] These activities, along with visits to the market to buy textiles from nearby villages, kept the two women busy.

On learning that Ledyard Smith was not planning to leave for their highland expedition for another two weeks, Tania took Alla to visit Lake Atitlán. They relaxed comfortably, and Tania once again enjoyed sketching the lake and volcanoes. They followed this with a day trip to Antigua and a longer visit to Quiriguá. During one of their evenings together in a hotel, Tania noted, "Mother is still writing endless postcards. She takes to tourism like a duck [to water]."[64] After weeks of traveling, Tania saw her mother off at the airport in Guatemala City. It had been a pleasant trip, and in the years ahead they shared other happy times traveling together.

Tania spent the next two days making sketches of a photograph Smith had brought back from the start of his field season. She bought supplies of canned goods and drugs her mother had suggested would be helpful on the expedition, then repacked for their departure. Smith and Tejeda loaded the luggage and equipment into the Carnegie truck, a secondhand ambulance that they named Elly, short for *elefante* (elephant). Put to the test on the steep, rugged roads of the Guatemalan highlands where elevations soar from 6,000 to 12,000 feet, Elly proved to be an endearing, though unpredictable workhorse.

On the first day out, they discovered Elly's brakes pulled to the left, locked up, and leaked fluid. Concerned about the treacherous mountain passes ahead of them, they decided to stop for repairs in Huehuetenango. While there, they paid a visit to nearby Zaculeu, a site the United Fruit Company had funded for excavation and reconstruction. They spent the day walking around the ruins with Boggs and Trik who were in charge of the project. It was a happy reunion with her old friends, and she was duly impressed with the site: "Mound 1 was so much as I imagined it that I almost thought I had been there before."[65] They also stopped in at the office to look over the array of pottery and artifacts found during excavation.

With Elly's repairs completed, they resumed their drive. In her diary, Tania described their ascent: "The climb across the Cuchumatanes

A. Ledyard Smith, undated. Courtesy of Ledyard and Jacqueline Smith.

mountain range is dramatic, steep and long. . . . Clouds were pouring across the mountains and we went up and up incredibly high toward these clouds. At the very top we had to drive through them, and the road became muddy and slippery with deep ruts where cars had passed."[66]

The mechanic's repairs did not hold for long: "The climb to Agua-catan was our Waterloo. . . . [T]here descended a cold fog and Elly balked for the second time. She lost her fan. We tried to adjust it but it just kept slipping off. . . . We decided finally to coast as far as possible and to ride until she bailed. Then we would stop and open a can of something to keep us cheerful, sleep a little and repeat the process. We rolled in . . . at midnight with one can of sardines left."[67]

Finally in Nebaj, the town that was to serve as their base for the duration of the field season, they set up quarters in a small pension run by the Migoya family. The ruins to be excavated were within walking distance of the pension on the property of a local butcher. Smith presented his permission papers to the town's mayor; then, to the landowner, he gave the shotgun he had brought from the United States just for this purpose. With these details taken care of, they walked out to survey the ruins.

Once the work routine was established, Smith left Tejeda in charge of the excavation and went with Tania to visit other ruins included in the survey. During the next several months, they made trips to more than twelve sites in the departments of Huehuetenango, Baja Verapaz, and Quiché. Getting to some of these sites, such as Huil and Chuitinamit, involved hours of driving over rough roads, securing a place to sleep, and riding on horseback in the early morning on steep trails through mountain passes. Often Tania had only several hours during the heat of the day in which to take the necessary measurements of the existing structures and to make sketches of the surrounding terrain and vegetation to use in her final reconstruction drawings.[68] She described returning from one site: "it is a long ride down the valley and I felt the saddle as ever. . . . I again had some trouble with the caballito which got away from me. . . . The descent is slow and even after we got below I began to doubt that my beastie would survive the journey. I decided it did not have a very happy home for it certainly was in no hurry to get there."[69]

To reach Xolchún, they had to hike several hours: "We had to wade across the Rio Blanco with water up to our knees. . . . One of our Indians was loathe to wade across because he claimed it gave him rheumatism, so the other rode him piggy-back while he hung on to my arm apparently afraid I'd be carried off by the current."[70]

In addition to these trips, Tania spent time at Nebaj where the excavations had revealed an altar and a series of vaulted tombs that spanned a period of more than seven hundred years. Although little standing architecture remained, primarily because of the region's extensive farming, she stayed busy with her drawings of the other sites. Walking

Tzicuay, Department of Quiché, Highlands Expedition, 1947, drawing by
Tania. Courtesy of President & Fellows of Harvard College, Peabody
Museum, Harvard University (N 34822).

to the dig each day, she also recorded positions of the newly discovered tombs and caches on the site plans.

In quiet moments, Tania enjoyed sketching the colorful market, church, and houses in the quaint town. Whenever she stopped to draw, chattering children gathered around her to watch. She bought a loom from a local woman and paid her for weaving lessons.[71] Her ability to communicate in Spanish improved greatly. As Smith later noted, "The one thing that really upset Tania was that our laborers who were able to speak some Spanish could understand my poor Spanish but not her excellent command of the language."[72] Such good-natured competitiveness was typical of Tania's relationships with many of her friends. Shook had once even suggested that she worked best alone, but her diary entries from this expedition indicate none of the irritation or impatience with her companions that she had felt at Copán. When Kidder sent word that her Salvador trip was canceled, she wrote, "I'm having too much fun here to be seriously disappointed."[73]

By April the weather turned colder, with frequent rains, making both travel and work on the dig more difficult. Among the townspeople there was an outbreak of measles and typhoid, and both Tania and Doug Binney, who had come to work when Tejeda returned to the university, came down with colds they could not shake off. Smith too became ill, suffering from an unexplained high fever accompanied by a bad rash of red welts. Tania brought out the medications her mother had put together for the expedition, and with these she did what she could to keep him comfortable. When his hands and feet began to swell and speech became difficult, they decided to drive to Guatemala City where a doctor could properly diagnose and treat the problem.[74] This marked the end of their field season, and as there was political unrest in the capital, Tania soon flew back to the United States.

The coming years would test their relationship, but reflecting on the expedition, Smith noted in 1985, "On all occasions Tania took without complaint the many discomforts that were encountered, principally poor living conditions in places where we had to stay and the frequent breakdowns of our car. . . . Tania was not only a good sport and a good companion but a great help at all times."[75]

Mayapán and the Demise of the Carnegie Division of Historical Research (1947–1958)

The return to Cambridge brought Tania back to the realities of the division's plight, and she felt increasing pressure to complete her manuscript on Maya art. She struggled with the text, but by November 1947 she finished her first draft. She noted in her diary, "I spent all day re-reading my manuscript. It is very raw in places but hangs together better than I thought." On the next reading, she reconsidered her assessment: "Thinking back over what I have read . . . it strikes me as something that could have been written over the weekend. I feel quite discouraged."[1] For years she had struggled with feelings of inadequacy about her writing, and it was a shortcoming she worked hard to overcome.

In January Tania gave her manuscript to the British Mayanist J. Eric S. Thompson for his suggestions. With more than seventy articles and books already to his credit, he was a key figure in Maya studies. Thompson was born in 1898 and, the son of a London doctor, was raised with the comforts and privileges of upper-middle-class English society. At the outbreak of World War I, though still young, he served his country in the trenches of Europe and was severely wounded. After the war he spent four years working as a gaucho on his family's estate in Argentina, then returned to England to complete his education at Cambridge University. It was here, while studying anthropology, that he first became fascinated with the Maya, particularly with their system of writing. Working with Morley's *Introduction to the Study of the Maya Hieroglyphs,* he taught himself how to compute Maya dates, a skill that got him a job at Chichén with the Carnegie Institution in 1926.[2]

Thompson worked with Morley in Yucatán for several years before accepting a position as an assistant curator for the Chicago Museum of Natural History. Nine years later he returned as a permanent staff member of the Carnegie, a position he retained until retiring. In 1948 Thompson was the editor of "Notes on Middle American Archaeology and Ethnology," a job Tania later assumed, and was in the process of completing a draft of his major work, *Maya Hieroglyphic Writing: An Introduction,* which would be published in 1950.

He was a complex man, strong-willed and opinionated. In his memoirs Shook described Thompson as "very close with all his data and information," not sharing his research until it had first been published under his own name. Shook suggested that although Thompson was brilliant, he was "arrogant and selfish."[3] Tania's relationship, and that of other scholars, with Thompson contrasted sharply with this view. They had already collaborated on an article titled "Maya Calendar Round Dates Such as 9 Ahau 17 Mol" published in 1947 by CIW. After going through the draft of her book at his home in Harvard, Massachusetts, Thompson responded warmly: "Dear Tanyuska . . . I have thoroughly enjoyed reading your ms., and derived much profit from it. . . . I can see that your results are going to be extremely useful for the epigraphist, and I am very glad that you did not pusseyfoot. . . . It is a swell piece of work, and opens up all kinds of inviting avenues. My heartiest congratulations."[4]

Kidder included a description of her project in his annual report on the work of the Historical Division: "Miss Tatiana Proskouriakoff has continued work on Maya sculptural art with special attention to the stelae of the Classic Period. . . . It has the double aim of tracing the development of Maya stone carving . . . and of determining objective criteria which will permit the dating of stelae and other sculptures that bear no inscriptions or inscriptions that have been so damaged as to resist decipherment."[5] Tania's work, though not yet published, was already receiving recognition, enhancing her stature in the division. No longer the shy, "relatively invisible"[6] female who had first set up a drafting table in the Carnegie offices in 1939, Tania had evolved into a vibrant and challenging colleague.

While working on the text for her book, Tania had continued to draw the reconstructions of highland sites for Smith's publication. In the same report, Kidder described this work as, "a series of restoration drawings, similar to those in her *Album of Maya Architecture* . . . with field sketches of the often very spectacular setting of the groups."[7] Though less known than those in her *Album*, these reconstructions are considered among her finest drawings.

Socially, Tania enjoyed regular evenings out with Ruppert and Smith. They went to see a play or a movie, then for dinner and drinks either at a local restaurant or at one of their apartments. Tania wrote, "I am invited to what has become our routine Monday date. I made them a proposition that I would pay for my ticket but was rejected."[8] The two men often entertained Tania with various card and magic tricks they had learned at the local adult education center, and they tempted her to join them for a class. Tania enjoyed the camaraderie of her colleagues and experienced a social period more akin to when she lived in Philadelphia.

Occasionally the group became a foursome with the addition of Kisa Noguchi, a talented drafter who was working on the line drawings for Tania's book. Kisa sometimes prepared sukiyaki for them after a day of combing through bookstores together. In the preface to her book, Tania acknowledged her friend's contribution: "Miss Kisa Noguchi has made all the line and rendered drawings that are the basis of the analysis forming the core of this book. Her infinite patience and truly remarkable accuracy in rendering Maya designs command my unreserved gratitude and admiration."[9] However, the presence of her friends in the office could sometimes be distracting: "I was finally off to a start on a better version of my text. . . . I got quite a bit accomplished before Karl, Ledyard and Kisa came in when I couldn't resist a brief interruption."[10]

The group's taste in theater was diverse and included *Show Boat* and Noel Coward's *Hay Fever*, which especially appealed to Tania. There were also times when Tania went to a concert or movie alone with Smith, after which they often stopped for drinks and conversation. After one evening together, Tania expressed concern for her friend: "I think he is restless and unsettled. The only time he really talks of what is on his mind is when he drinks too much, and his reticence makes me shy."[11]

Smith was an attractive, eligible divorcé, and the two enjoyed each other's company. Tania would soon be turning forty, and friends began to speculate about what she should do about her private life. After dinner with a couple she saw regularly, she wrote, "I rather enjoyed the evening even though Ed Hale ragged me about getting married. . . . It seems to be the conversation for this month."[12] It would not be the last of such ragging.

Marriage was also a topic for Smith and his son at this time. "Junior," as Tania referred to him in her diaries, was a young impressionable boy when he first went with his father to the Carnegie office in Cambridge. In an interview, he recalled feeling intimidated on meeting Tania. He thought this was in part because his father had so often described her as brilliant and in part because she seemed cold and aloof. The boy may have perceived the ambiguity in his father's relationship with Tania and the uncertainty of what role she might play in his life.[13]

However, for reasons Tania never understood, the balance in the Monday night group shifted. One week neither Smith nor Ruppert showed up to go to the theater, and later Tania wrote, "Karl hurt my feelings by a frontal attack and I was glum for two days. Afterwards he pretended that nothing had happened, but I think something has. . . . Ledyard's confidences under the influence of slightly too much drink . . . showed me the real care behind the attitudes [and] have never been repeated in sobriety. Perhaps he never intended to make them."[14] As was her custom, she insulated herself from hurt by throwing herself into her work, attending lectures, and reading. The books she read at this time included Toscano's *El arte pre-columbiano* and Leonid Strakhanisky's *Life of Alexander I*.

After a whirlwind romance, Smith remarried. His bride was Katharine Moss Mellon, a woman he had met recently at a party. "Kitty" wrote a column for the *New York World-Telegram*, but after the wedding, she quit her job and devoted herself to being Smith's wife and companion.[15] In the coming years, Kitty often went into the field, helping in various capacities. The 1949 *Carnegie Institution Year Book* report on Smith's fieldwork in the Guatemala highlands bore similarities to the season Tania had shared just the year before. During this field season, Tania remained in Cambridge, working on her book on Maya art. In her diary she wrote, "I wasted the rest of the day reading Landa, listening to *La Boheme* and missing L."[16] Later she added, "I have been rather sad because neither Ledyard nor Karl seems to want to know me now. I do not know why. With Ledyard it is probably because his wife and I have not hit it off."[17] While Tania had opportunities in the coming years to improve relations with Kitty, she did not choose to do so. Kitty died of cancer in the mid-1950s, leaving Smith to raise their child, Camilla, along with his son and daughter from a previous marriage. Through their continuing work, Tania and Smith were able to overcome the distance that had developed between them, but their relationship had become that of working colleagues.

Tania now went through a period of depression similar to ones she had experienced earlier at Copán and during the war years. In her diary she confided, "The last two years have been a bleak period . . . of discouragement and disappointment and a search for some new sustaining philosophy. I have felt loneliness and thwarted desires. Now I feel on an even keel, but it may just be a reaction from having hit bottom and bobbing up again."[18] Later she wrote, "I have been very unhappy and have pulled out of it on, as it were, a higher plane. It is apparent that none of my personal desires or ambitions will be gratified. . . . I don't know yet if I were free to choose whether I would take the comradeship of a social life or the terrific loneliness that I'm apparently doomed to suffer."[19] This question would continue to haunt Tania periodically in the years ahead.

Many factors may have contributed to Tania's depression. One was the death of her longtime friend and mentor, Morley. Kidder wrote, "With Morley's death on September 2, 1948, the Maya, ancient and modern, lost their most tireless and effective advocate."[20] Tania also had lost an advocate in Morley, one who had a tremendous impact on her life and career. It was Morley who first brought Tania to the attention of the Carnegie Institution, and it was he who envisioned a book of her reconstruction drawings that resulted in her first major publication, *An Album of Maya Architecture*. When she was disheartened in her early years with the Carnegie, it was Morley she turned to for inspiration and encouragement. Finally, it was a friendly disagreement with him over the dating of a monument that resulted in her current project on Maya art. This was not, however, the only loss for Tania during this time.

Six months before this, Tania grieved over the death of one of the foremost leaders of the twentieth century, a man for whom she felt deep admiration. In 1948 a Hindu, opposed to Mohandas Gandhi's policy of appeasement and nonviolence, shot and killed him. Tania wrote, "Gandhi seems to me to be the last great figure of a great age. No one at all approaches him in stature on the modern scene."[21] In a later reflection on his death, she wrote, "I have mourned for three public men: Gandhi, Roosevelt and Will Rogers." Rogers was a plainspoken political humorist who during the depression had suggested the government should hire unemployed workers by sponsoring massive public works projects.[22] It was the sort of practical politics Tania respected.

Also contributing to this dark period in Tania's life was the current political atmosphere in which the cold war between the United States and the Soviet Union was heating up. Tania wrote, "Now that Truman has committed us to open antagonism against Russia it looks as if another war is inevitable. I've thought a lot about it and I have decided no longer to stand on principle. . . . If opportunity offers I will probably join in . . . and think as little as possible. If one thinks or cares it is too tragic to bear."[23] On August 29, 1949, the Soviet Union detonated its first atomic bomb, altering what sense of security remained for the American public. Citizens volunteered for Operation Skywatch and with binoculars scanned the skies for Soviet bombers. Harry Truman, pursuing a policy of containment of the Soviet threat, called on Congress to substantially build up the nation's conventional and nuclear forces.[24] Tania wrote, "Even the best of us don't seem to be able to think without a glance over the shoulder at the specter of communism."[25] This was only the beginning of the "Red" hysteria of the 1950s.

In spite of her depressed state, this was a productive period for Tania professionally. Her manuscript on Maya art was nearly completed, and men like Kidder and Thompson were supporting her efforts. Alfred Tozzer, another of the preeminent figures in Middle American anthropology and archaeology, now played an important role in Tania's life. Thirty years her senior and recently retired from his position as the John E. Hudson Professor of Archaeology at Harvard, Tozzer maintained an office in the Peabody Museum and often looked in on the Carnegie offices next door.[26] Known to love a good debate, he regularly stopped to talk with Tania, sometimes inviting her to continue their discussions at his home nearby at 7 Bryant Street. Over cocktails, graciously served by his wife, these conversations both stimulated and inspired Tania.

In January 1949 Tania described with pleasure one of their discussions: "Another mad session with Tozzer this morning. I think I have convinced him that there's some foundation to my remarks on Yucatán, though he still resists the idea of non-Classic Maya deriving their traits from abroad. It was fun." The next day, he invited her to his office: "He then offered me some of his pamphlets and ended up by giving me his Landa, *The Maya and Their Neighbors*, Bowditch and a number of Peabody Papers, almost a library! It is so good of him and I value the encouragement more than anything else."[27] These gifts prompted Tania to buy a new bookcase for her apartment and to catalog and arrange her growing collection of books.

Tania took time out from her increasingly busy schedule to visit Kay and her family in Portland. Before her departure, she wrote, "I hope I can use my vacation as a springboard for a better ordered life, and particularly more discrimination in reading. Most of the time it is a means of escape from loneliness and from more difficult tasks."[28] Her itinerary allowed for a stopover in Chicago to see an exhibition at the Chicago Art Institute. She described her visit in her diary: "Their collection of post-impressionists is splendid particularly Matisse, Utrillo, Braque and even some fine Americans. . . . I spotted, too, a good Orozco who is my favorite of the Mexicans."[29]

Tania's weeks in Portland were restful. She visited quietly with her sister and became reacquainted with her niece and nephew whom she had not seen in years. Alla was also visiting, and she and Tania traveled back home on the scenic Trans-Canadian railroad. In her thank-you letter, Tania wrote, "[T]he views of the Canadian Rockies were magnificent and when the train stopped we would get out to sniff the mountain air and look at the Swiss chalets they have planted here and there." Their only difficulty occurred at the border: "The immigration officer growled at us because we didn't have any papers—but there we were on the train and apparently he didn't want to waste his energies throwing us off."[30] They arrived in Boston tired but happy, in a sweltering heat wave, the last of the summer. Soon after, Alla returned to Philadelphia. The days began to cool, and students once again swarmed Harvard Square.

Earlier that year Tania had worked hard preparing the prints for her book, *A Study of Classic Maya Sculpture*, and she received the edited manuscript from the staff publication editor. In her self-effacing way, Tania found it merely "O.K." After the addition of a preface, the book went to press. In his yearly report, Kidder related the publication of Tania's book to that of Thompson's on hieroglyphs: "Each serves to round out the more general study of the Maya on which the Division has so long been engaged, and each lays firm foundations for work on these important aspects of Maya culture during the later stages that will be under investigation by the Division in future years."[31] Later, Satterthwaite reacted to the book by letter: "[I]t is as important as rumour had it, and a hell of a fine job. I can see why it took quite a while." He added, "There is this one complaint. I haven't been able to figure out how to construct the graphs. . . . I'm not carping, I really want to know how to use the system."[32] After some clarification, he worked with her style-dating system and assigned a graduate student, Ann Chowning, to use it to date the museum's recently acquired stela. He conveyed this to Tania: "[Chowning's] net result is precisely what you got, and agrees with an almost sure reading of the inscription. My admiration for that job rises constantly."[33]

With her book completed, Tania relaxed during the Christmas holidays with Alla and her aunt Mila's family in Philadelphia. She also took the train to Washington and New York to catch up with old friends. This included a visit with Josephine Suddards, her dearest friend from high school days. Married to Marsh McCall, a cardiologist, "Jo" lived with her husband and children in a large apartment on Park Avenue. Tania stayed with them, sitting up late into the night with her friend, smoking, talking, and laughing. This connection remained important to Tania in the years ahead, and the McCall children grew up calling her by her childhood nickname, Duchess. Jo's son, Marsh, attended Harvard and later became a professor in the classics department at Stanford University. In an interview, he recalled the affection his family felt for Tania and said that she had encouraged and inspired him to excel when he was a student.[34]

After the holidays Tania finalized her plans to travel to Mexico City and Veracruz in search of a new research project. To her sister, she wrote, "I am in the midst of preparations for my trip south. Inoculations, photographs, police certificates. But the worst is getting clothes together. For all the times I've been there I have never worked out an efficient wardrobe, since it is cold in the mountains and hot as Hades below and you're passing from winter to summer in one suitcase as well as from muleback to city."[35] After reserving a seat on a flight, she reflected, "Strangely enough though I distrust our diabolical machines I feel no apprehension. Perhaps at my age one begins to feel that he has achieved about all that he's likely to. That from now on it is denouement, and that few problems will be solved in the years that are left. . . . Perhaps I have been after all lucky in escaping personal happiness and in being forced against my natural inclination to live alone."[36] She did not realize that her most productive years were still to come.

In Mexico City she took a room downtown at a hotel just off the historic central square overlooking the busy Avenida Madero. Her room was noisy, but it was bright, cheerful, and conveniently located across from Sanborn's, an old establishment where travelers and locals often met for afternoon coffee and pastries or a comfortable meal. She called Bodil Christensen, who came for tea, filling Tania in on the changes around the city since her last visit. Tania wrote, "She seems to know everything that goes on in Mexico, particularly in archaeology. We had supper together too, and the day seemed very short."[37]

Tania spent the next days at the Museo Nacional, where she enjoyed a hearty reception from the employees who remembered her from earlier visits. She stayed busy with meetings at the museum and the Instituto, day trips to Teotihuacán, and viewing private art collections. Her evenings were filled with dinner parties and dancing. Of her time in the city, she observed, "Mexico seems one moment gay and the next sordid. Poverty intrudes on the prosperity of the main streets. The taste of the rich shops is higher than anything we have in the States, and one is tempted by beautiful materials and designs. Leather and silver are everywhere—and very good things, too."[38]

This hectic schedule left Tania exhausted, with a case of dysentery and a bad cold. Irritated that she had succumbed to illness, she wrote, "How awful to be such a damn inefficient organism."[39] After several days' rest, she caught a bus out of the capital, crossing the eastern mountains to the tropical lowlands of Veracruz where she was to meet with the archaeologist in charge of work at El Tajín. She stayed at a small hotel in Jalapa and dined several times at the archaeologist's home. She wrote, "García Payón was more than cordial, but I didn't get much out of him. . . . The only thing accomplished is an arrangement to go to Tajín on the 20th."[40] In a postcard to her sister, she wrote, "I am battling perpetual colds, but otherwise the trip has been fun so far. Next week I go into the jungles and am going to camp alone for several days."[41] Tania returned to photograph the ruins, though whether she went alone or with a group, is unclear.[42] Her diary entries for the remainder of her stay in Mexico are sporadic and moody. Frustrated by her physical condition and by a sense that she "was infringing on other people's territory,"[43] Tania abandoned her intentions of finding a new research project in Mexico and made the return trip home by train.

After some weeks back at the unusually quiet Carnegie offices, she wrote, "As the novelty of being home wears off, the feeling of loneliness and futility steals back on me. I am determined, however, not to yield to it again, and to enjoy as far as possible what is yet left to be enjoyed."[44] In this spirit Tania once again began attending concerts, plays, and lectures with various friends. On one of these evenings, she heard a speech by Alexander Kerensky, once leader of the provisional government formed in 1916 after the abdication of Czar Nicholas: "He struck me as a tragic figure—probably the most tragic one can conceive—a man to whom chance delivered an unbounded opportunity—and who was unequal to it. . . . He orates, he shouts, he whispers dramatically—but he doesn't say anything. . . . How very sad that such tremendous responsibilities fall, more often perhaps than we think, on the shoulders of middling men."[45]

She also began attending meetings of the Civil Liberties Union of Massachusetts. Here she found people with common ideals, who were concerned by the atmosphere of bitter mistrust that Senator Joseph McCarthy was generating in the House Un-American Activities Committee. In a letter to her sister, she wrote, "That outfit has a lot of interesting people in it, but unfortunately one doesn't get to know them just sitting around listening to speeches, and I haven't time to volunteer as a stamp-licker."[46] Later, she wrote in her diary, "It is easier to understand the terror inspired by despotic governments when such things are happening here. . . . [T]he persecutions continue. . . . It is apparently no longer safe to hold liberal opinions and all out hate for communists is a requisite for any public activity."[47]

The sword rattling between the United States and the Soviet Union worried many, including Tania: "The crisis is intensifying everyday. We expect war-time 'controls' to be announced on Friday. . . . I don't see how a major conflict can be avoided." Disturbed by the quality of leadership in the country, she continued, "What can one expect? President Truman in a letter to a reporter who criticized his daughter Margaret's singing offered to punch his nose, and the fool promptly published it. . . . Men whose personal behavior is not up to the social standards of civilized life can hardly be expected to lead their nations in a peaceful and dignified way."[48]

In some way, however, Tania was energized by this political climate. At times she felt "supremely alive,"[49] and her diary entries consistently suggest she was becoming more outgoing in her relationships. In one example she recounts a discussion that began innocently among several people in the office, describing that one "touched on his 'occult' experiences in Peru and the 'emanations' that meet him as he enters 10 Frisbie.

Somehow Mu and Atlantis came into it too." She continued, "[Another colleague] countered by offering a story of her own on a 'transcendent' or 'psychic' experience and I found myself in an intense argument I had never intended to start. . . . It isn't only idle hands that get into mischief."[50] On another occasion she described her visit to the Peabody next door: "A blonde little squirt from Social Relations was spouting off about archaeologists and their love for digging holes which are symbols of their mother's womb. What rubbish clutters their heads! Kluckhohn was angrily shuffling papers, Izabel was giggling and Coe shouting forth—a very sociable place that museum. . . . Something on a play asks to be written."[51] Over the years Tania periodically toyed with plots for short stories and considered the idea of supporting herself by writing fiction.

She was also spending more time in serious discussions with Tozzer. After one meeting, she wrote, "He as usual was leaping far ahead of me in every direction. . . . He has been reading me his reconstruction of Yucatán history. His power of collating and synthesizing miscellaneous, often contradictory, data is truly remarkable. He flatters me by the long quotes he makes from my book and the Yucatán paper."[52] Tozzer delighted in sparring with the younger woman, and it was stimulating for them both.

A job Tania took on at this time was drafting the design for a medal in honor of Kidder's impending retirement. In his name, the American Anthropological Association established an award to be given every three years for outstanding contributions in the fields of southwestern U.S. archaeology and Mesoamerican archaeology. On one side of the disk, Tania drew the Cliff Palace at Mesa Verde, New Mexico; on the other, she reproduced a scene of two Maya lords in profile from a plaque unearthed in Kaminaljuyu.[53] Both sites were important in Kidder's long, illustrious career. In a letter to her sister, Tania confided, "The guys that are making the A.V.K. medal are . . . fooling around unnecessarily long. . . . I tried to put the fear of God into them and underline the deadline."[54] As reported in the *Boston Herald*, one hundred of the cast-bronze medals were ordered, enough to last until the year 2250.[55] Presented in December 1950, the first recipient was Kidder's

The A. V. Kidder Medal, depicting Cliff Palace, Mesa Verde, New Mexico, designed by Tania and awarded to her in 1962. Medal on loan from Mike Beetem. Photo courtesy of Tom Oakley.

longtime colleague, Alfred M. Tozzer. Although Tania said she did not wish to be paid for her work on the medal, she received a check for $300. She later wrote to her sister, "I told the committee that the design was strictly on me, but they apparently didn't know what to do with the surplus. . . . I can't very well throw it back at them."[56] Satterthwaite sent a letter to compliment her on the design: "Your mother loaned me your copy of the Kidder medal to show off around here. It is a beautiful thing, and fills me with pride to remember that I knew you when."[57]

Tania now prepared to leave for her field season in Yucatán, a routine she followed for the next five years. She arranged for a friend to stay in her apartment while she was away. She got her shots and made

The A. V. Kidder Medal, depicting a piece from Kaminaljuyu, Guatemala, designed by Tania. Photo courtesy of Tom Oakley.

reservations for the train to Miami, where she would visit her old friends, the Polevitzskys. Like Tania, Igor Polevitzsky was born in czarist Russia, left with his parents at the time of the revolution, and became a naturalized American citizen. He studied for a degree in architecture, and by 1951 he had a thriving architectural firm that specialized in hotels such as the Shelborne and the Albion in Miami Beach. Tania's visits were cause for celebration. Meeting her at the train station, Polevitzsky and his wife, Irene, kept Tania in a constant flurry of activities. They took her out for dinner and drinks, then to the racetrack where Tania placed a frugal bet. After she had seen his office and latest designs, she wrote, "Igor is really doing fine stuff. . . . [H]e took me to see some of his buildings and I was very much impressed by their simple effectiveness."[58] This was just one of many visits she made over the years to see her "scattered friends." Her friendships mattered deeply to Tania. Besides the Polevitzskys, she remained close to the Satterthwaites and the McCalls, as well as her college friend, Polly Margolf. After this hectic visit in Miami, she flew on to Mérida, where more close friends, the Shooks, met her. This would be their base of operations for the coming months as they prepared for their long-term project at the site of Mayapán.

Under pressure from the CIW president, the staff of the Division of Historical Research, now under the direction of Pollock and renamed the Department of Archaeology, had agreed, after much debate, to refocus its combined talents. Kidder suggested before his retirement that their "future effort . . . should be . . . a shift from a general study of the Maya past to . . . an intensive study of the protohistoric period of northern Yucatán."[59] Although Mayapán met the requirements for the proposed time period, it aroused little enthusiasm and proved to be the Carnegie's last venture into archaeology.

In the first field season, a building was leased in Mérida to serve as the project's main office and storage headquarters. Tania and Shook worked closely there, sorting and cataloging the large collections of archaeological artifacts that had accumulated over the years from various Carnegie projects. These included bones, sculpture, and pottery that had been stored in approximately five hundred boxes just outside Mérida at Hacienda Chenkú. In an agreement with the Instituto Nacional de Antropología e Historia, suitable specimens were to be delivered to the Mérida Museum at the end of the season.[60]

Strömsvik too was often in town to buy supplies, as he was in charge of renovating a building a short distance from the ruins that would serve as living and working quarters for the large staff during excavations. This was located in the village of Telchaquillo, a bone-jarring two-and-a-half-hour drive from Mérida over rough, pitted roads. Smith and Ruppert stayed in these unfinished quarters while conducting a survey of the standing remains at the site.

Settling into a comfortable routine, the months, though hot, passed pleasantly for Tania. In her off-hours, she enjoyed gossiping with Señora

Sketch of CIW headquarters at Telchaquillo, Yucatán, Mexico, by Tania, undated. Courtesy of President &

Cámara, matron of the household where Tania and others with the Carnegie had rooms. She liked to walk to the main *zócalo*, the Plaza de Independencia, to sketch the impressive cathedral and the S-shaped benches that grace many parks of Yucatán.[61] There were the usual gatherings of American archaeologists, passing through on their way to their own projects, and cocktail parties in the evenings with friends in the Mexican archaeological community such as Alberto Ruz. Spontaneous get-togethers often took place in the bar at the Gran Hotel or nearby at Fernando Barbachano's Hotel Mérida, where drinks were plentiful and conversations rich with ideas and tales of adventure.

At the end of the 1951 field season, Tania returned to Cambridge, resolved to make the most of her year, in spite of the unrest caused by the war in Korea and the uncertainty of the department's future. In a transitional period and still looking for some new direction that would capture her interest, she went in daily to the office. There was a palpable atmosphere of tension, with everyone under pressure to produce publications on their previous projects, some of which had been started years before. Pollock, adjusting to his new position as the department's director, confided in Tania his concerns about personality conflicts.[62] He delegated to her the responsibility of gathering and editing the notes from her colleagues on their year's activities for the Carnegie *Year Book*. It was sometimes a trying task and placed Tania in a delicate position with her colleagues.

Just one example was dealing with Shook, whose written report was months late. Tania, working on a strict deadline, became increasingly concerned. Without this report, the summer trip she had been planning since the previous Christmas was in jeopardy. Asked to present a paper at an international conference in Jalapa, she had invited her mother and an old friend, Katusha Zworykin, to drive with her to Mexico. They wanted to take several weeks, sharing the sights and colorful village markets en route. When the tardy report finally arrived, their trip proceeded as planned.

The women were excellent traveling companions. In the years since her last trip, Alla had earnestly studied Spanish and was now able to converse comfortably with the locals in the markets she so loved. She showed great physical stamina and was excited by the new places she had the opportunity to visit. Shook joined them in Mexico City, driving with them across the mountains to Jalapa, where he and Tania participated in the conference. From there, the three women drove to Oaxaca, finding it "spectacular."[63] Tania met with the Mexican artist Miguel Covarrubias and saw his extensive collection of Mexican antiquities. Like his close friend, the muralist Diego Rivera, many women found Covarrubias charming and magnetic. In a letter to the Shooks, Tania described this visit: "The man is badly run after, for which I must confess I can't blame anybody much. When I called him he told me he wasn't there and didn't know when he would be back, but on hearing my name he said *that* was different—he was right there all the time." In the lighthearted, familiar tone typical of many of her letters to the Shooks, she concluded that the woman Covarrubias had been avoiding apparently caught up with him later.[64]

After more than a month on the road, Tania returned to the United States by train while the two older women drove back at a more leisurely pace. It was the last time Tania and her mother traveled together. Reflecting on the trip, Alla wrote in her monthly letter to Kay, "Tania and the car made the trip what it was—most interesting and worthwhile—we got into places where the tourists do not go and saw real Mexico unspoiled." In a poignant tribute to her daughters for whom she had been a strong role model as a doctor, wife, and mother, she added, "Both you and Tania are my pride and joy, and I don't know what I did to deserve such brilliant daughters."[65]

Tania spent the next Christmas with her mother in Philadelphia. She described the visit to her sister: "We had a wild and very gay time in, what with AAAS meeting and holiday festivities. Mother doesn't seem to mind my bringing in mobs of archys for her to feed."[66] Alla was more specific in her own letter: "There were meetings of Association for [the] Advancement of Science and a lot of out of town archaeologists and anthropologists were floating around. Tania wanted to give a party and we had 18 people for cocktails and buffet supper. Can you imagine such a crowd in my two-room apartment? It took a lot of planning and careful cooking! But the party was quite a success."[67]

Tania returned to Cambridge to prepare herself for another season in Yucatán. Shortly thereafter, she traveled by train with Pollock from Boston to New Orleans, where they conferred with Robert Wauchope, head of Tulane University's Middle American Research Institute. They then flew into Mérida. "It all seems so familiar—as if I were here only two weeks ago!" Tania wrote. She checked in at the office, finding it in excellent shape, then walked back to her hotel to dress for a date with Strömsvik, fearing that once again it would "not come off." When he failed to show up, she had dinner instead with "the crowd including Kitty and the Gutiérrez."[68]

Completing their final preparations, the staff departed for field headquarters in CIW vehicles. Tania described their arrival in Telchaquillo:

> It is a sprawling, wide-streeted town which seems to have no particular reason for existing. The plaza is just a space with a ruined roofless church at one end. . . . One enters through an arched driveway into a yard which is of the same Yucatecan rock one sees everywhere. . . . The original one room house serves as dining room and office. Behind this room is a kitchen, a bodega, and servants' quarters. On the other side of the driveway is a row of rooms facing back on a wide porch and my room in an ell projecting backward. . . . I have two comfortable beds, two chairs, a square table and a chest of four deep drawers. . . . One almost forgets that nothing is available but what one has brought.[69]

Early the next day Tania went with the others in the truck to inspect the ruins. She found the overcast conditions "simply ideal for tromping around." Later she showered and went for a walk in the town: "Though the houses are simple thatched huts, most yards are kept neat and here and there at great cost of labor, tiny gardens are constructed. Fruit trees and native cotton grow in the yards." She ran into Romalda, assistant to the project's cook, who offered to show her around. Together they went to see the town's cenote and then to the home of Romalda's cousin. Tania told the women that she wanted to learn to speak Maya and enjoyed their giggles when she attempted to repeat certain words. The next day Romalda left her a beautiful bouquet on the table in her bedroom.

Tania went daily to the ruins, working in various capacities. She felt frustrated and at loose ends, without a clear idea of what she should focus on for the field season. She wrote, "Time hangs heavy on my hands and I don't know whether to start a dig or record sculptures. Never have I so longed for an idea!"[70] In February she received a troubling letter from her mother stating that she had been ill and near a nervous breakdown. Tania wrote, "The letter is 10 days old and I am seriously worried for it is full of bad spelling and unusually sprawly."[71]

Her worries were justified. On a visit to her in-laws' house, Alla suddenly collapsed, as she was ringing the doorbell. Mila and her husband rushed her to the hospital, where the doctors found she had a tumor in the frontal lobe of her brain. Although the operation was performed by Philadelphia's foremost neurosurgeon, he was unable to remove the entire tumor.[72] When she was well enough to travel, Kay brought her mother to her home in Oregon where Tania, who flew in from Mexico, joined them. Six weeks later, Tania wrote, "I am going back to the job tomorrow—but it is hard to leave. A lifetime seems to have passed since I was in Telchaquillo and the dread of what is ahead and not being here is oppressive. . . . I can't bear to think that this may be the last time I see her."[73]

Tania returned to Yucatán and struggled through the remainder of the field season. In a dark moment she wrote, "The mood of depression settled deeper this evening—but it's a fool's game. I have a curious feeling of remoteness from this place and from everyone here. One has to go one's own way. Dependence on others is illusory. . . . The sympathy one finds in families and in rare friends takes years to mature and isn't scattered here and there."[74] When the Carnegie work at Mayapán wound down for the year, Tania flew to New Orleans and from there traveled by train to Boston. She was relieved to get home.

Less than a month later, Tania packed her papers and headed back to Oregon, where she could work while being near her mother. Alla's condition had deteriorated, and time dragged for the two sisters. Their once elegant mother was no longer able to sit and knit and was unaware if she stained her blouse. Tania wrote, "The vigil goes on. K thinks that mother is unaware that she is dying, but sometimes there is such a sad look on her face. . . . I feel enclosed and weighted down and unable to think of any place but that one dimly lighted room and mother's right hand . . . that flutters up and falls again on her chest. How can it last so long!"[75]

There were some attempts at normalcy. Tania worked on drawings, and she took her nephew with her when she flew to meet with the ethnohistorian Ralph Roys. Kay's husband took the family on a fishing trip to the coast, which lifted all their spirits. However, these were only brief periods of relief from the tensions of waiting and watching, as their mother's condition steadily declined.

Two months after Tania's arrival, Alla quietly passed away in a bedroom in her daughter's home. Tania wrote, "It is all over—very suddenly somehow. Mother died at 1:45 yesterday morning—completely unconscious and alone. . . . That day we had a simple ceremony . . . with pink roses and Chopin and even the conventional Christian words had no incongruity. . . . I couldn't help crying a little. . . . I shall miss her greatly."[76] Since her father's death, Tania's relationship with Alla had grown much deeper. Her loss affected Tania's life on many levels.

Returning East, Tania stopped in Philadelphia to see her aunt Mila, who had carefully stored Alla's belongings. They began to sort through them, deciding what should be given away and what should be kept in the family. She also made a final visit to the cottage at Spray Beach, where there had been so many happy family gatherings. She wrote, "The remembrance of her follows everything."[77] She arranged for the sale of the beach property, and on returning home to Cambridge, she made out a new will, naming her sister as her beneficiary.

That fall Tania spent considerable time with friends. She visited the Hales at their spacious home in Manchester, New Hampshire, describing the area as "beautiful coast with rocks and gulls and a quiet sea."[78] She spent restful days sketching and sailing in the cove and in a letter to the Satterthwaites wrote, "I second Peggy on the beauty of that coast, though I don't think I should care to have one of those little twelve-bedroom cottages there."[79] At home she enjoyed dinners with friends and evenings at the symphony.

Tania was productive at work. She completed a paper titled "The Survival of the Maya Tun Count in Colonial Times," which she sent to

Satterthwaite for his suggestions. It was published by the CIW in "Notes on Middle American Archaeology and Ethnology." She also submitted a paper, "Varieties of Classic Veracruz Sculpture," to the Carnegie publications editor, and it was published in volume 12 of *Contributions to American Anthropology and History*.[80] In spite of this busy writing schedule, Tania made time to do some drawings of stingray spines at Satterthwaite's request and to get to Philadelphia for the annual anthropological meetings held between Christmas and New Year's Eve.

She learned that Satterthwaite and Gordon R. Willey, who had taken over Tozzer's position at the Peabody, would be visiting Yucatán in the approaching season en route to their project in British Honduras. Hoping to find inspiration, Tania wrote Satterthwaite, "I am awfully glad you are coming to Mayapán. Maybe you can give us some ideas. I will be back at my old job of mapping, but I will need something more to keep me busy between seasons. Maybe you will see something in those rocks that I am missing."[81]

Tania once again headed to Yucatán. Dave De Harport, a Harvard graduate student in anthropology who was to work at Chichén,[82] accompanied her. In New Orleans before their flight to Mérida, she wrote, "The St. Charles, impressive as it is downstairs, has dingy old rooms and an appalling maze of hallways. Well—all that is minor annoyances. If I were enthusiastic about the job this season it could be taken in stride. The real trouble is somewhere in the background."[83] This foreboding was shared by others on the staff and became more apparent as the season progressed.

Tania spent a week at Chichén getting De Harport settled in to his work. She then returned to Mérida, where she met with the rest of the Carnegie staff. Together they headed to Telchaquillo, Strömsvik and Tania driving one vehicle, and Ruppert and Smith following behind in the truck. In the months since they had last traveled this road, heavy rains had washed away much of the roadbed, leaving large, exposed rocks. Exhausted from the long, bumpy ride, they found their staff waiting at the gate of the Carnegie headquarters. Tania described their greeting: "Karl lifts Parela off her feet and hugs her. Lucio and Guardelio are here too grinning from ear to ear. Everyone busies himself unpacking the trucks. We inspect the . . . back yard: . . . the Ramón tree twice as big as last year, the big and the little papayas, the poor dead Dama de Noche and the ailing tomatoes. . . . Gus and I chat about the new water purification system and test the scales. . . . We have a drink and are soon called in to supper."[84] It was a simple beginning to a complex season.

Pollock assigned Tania the task of conducting a comparative architectural study by making a large-scale plan of Mayapán's main ceremonial center. Clearing had already begun in earnest. In her *Year Book* report covering this field season, Tania wrote, "Because of the height of the constructions and their crowded arrangement, direct measurements were often difficult to obtain, and the project involved a resurvey of the entire group."[85] Tania was assisted by Bernardino Euan, a sixteen-year-old Maya, whom she trained and found quick to learn. When he was not needed, Euan occupied himself by shooting pebbles from a sling and catching lizards and snakes. Her fondness for the young man grew, and later she saw to it that he had the opportunity to attend school in Mérida and Mexico City, where he studied accounting. With Tania's backing, he eventually opened a small store of his own in Mérida. Euan periodically wrote her warm, respectful letters, and in 1981 he suggested that his daughter come to stay with her to help with whatever she might need. Though Tania did not accept, the offer was a reminder to the aging woman of the special connection made in Yucatán many years before.[86]

The daily routine for the staff at Mayapán began with breakfast at six o'clock, after which they went to the ruins. They worked in their respective areas until the midafternoon heat stopped most strenuous activities. Boxed lunches and thermoses of hot coffee helped them get through this long stretch of work, although the sight of buzzards circling overhead was disconcerting.[87] The number of staff members swelled with the arrival of Shook, Robert Smith, and Robert Adams. Soon everyone began to fall ill. Iodine in the water purification system was hard on their stomachs, leaving many out of sorts and irritable.[88]

Pollock, Satterthwaite, Willey, and a graduate student, Jerry Epstein, arrived later. In an interview Epstein recalled the bumpy ride from Mérida, sitting surrounded by hay in the back of a truck. When the truck came to a stop in the compound, Epstein fell out, and to his chagrin, the

CIW staff at Mayapán, 1953. Standing, left to right: Robert Adams, Ed Shook, Ledyard Smith, Harry Pollock, Ralph Roys. Seated, left to right: Bill Bullard, Gus Strömsvik, Tania, Robert Smith, David de Harport.

bottle of vodka he had been given for safekeeping fell to the ground and broke.[89] The staff were disappointed over the broken bottle, as most evenings they gathered for drinks before dinner. Generally, each poured a drink from his own bottle, but guests often brought a special bottle to be shared. Tania described the conversations during the cocktail hour as "a great deal of talk—most of it archaeological though none of it so far had led to new ideas."[90] By 9:00 P.M., most of the staff had retired to their rooms, and though Tania had fully intended to do some writing there, the schedule left her just enough energy to read her Maya primer.

With the uncertainty of the department's fate and so many personalities staying under one roof, tensions naturally arose. As he had done earlier in Guatemala during the war, Shook organized a softball game between the men at camp and the village. It proved to be a great success, easing tension and establishing closer ties with the people of Telchaquillo.[91] Tania enjoyed watching the games. She wrote, "It is refreshing to think of something besides Mayapán or geography. Too much of it is too much. I can now see why Ed and Ledyard take up baseball."[92] In the 1955 field season, the archaeologists sponsored uniforms for the local team, and Tania described their visit to headquarters: "Yesterday we had a delegation of baseball players who came to show off their new uniforms. Lots of red and blue. 'Reyes de Mayapán.' It is quite touching."[93]

Work progressed steadily, but nerves became more frayed. Frustrated, Tania wrote in her diary, "I am chiefly deterred by a complete blankness of mind, but to some small extent by the outbursts that accompany any remark that has a tinge of criticism, even when it is innocent and impersonal. . . . And the heat. That of course is the real monster."[94] Another factor contributing to the staff's irritability was interrupted sleep. A local bus made regular midnight stops in the village, blowing its horn repeatedly to give notice of its arrival. As passengers boarded, many carried with them loud, squealing pigs to be sold at the market. The intense heat of the afternoon hours prevented the Carnegie staff from taking a nap to catch up on lost sleep.[95]

Tania's friendships with Shook and Strömsvik remained strong, though Strömsvik continued his bouts of heavy drinking. It was with

Pollock that Tania seemed to feel the greatest tension. While their relationship had gone through periods of varying intensity, Tania walked a fine line with him. As director of the faltering department, Pollock experienced tremendous pressures and turned to her for support and ideas. However, at the end of the season, what Tania called the "final storm" occurred. One night, villagers came to the Carnegie headquarters to ask for a ride to locate some missing musicians who were to play for the boarhead dance in honor of the departing archaeologists. She wrote, "The typical reaction—'tell them we are about to go in to dinner'—seemed a bit cool and ungracious." She offered to go if Shook accompanied her: "Ed was willing but I was not permitted to go. This last attack on my independence has really brought things to a head. I can't permit it. The necessity to find an independent project becomes acute. Another season of this would be unsupportable."[96] There would be more problems for these two in the years ahead.

In spite of her intentions, Tania did not develop an independent project. Early the next season Pollock made a formal announcement to his staff of the decision by CIW president Vannevar Bush to liquidate the Department of Archaeology. While Shook took a leave of absence to lead the University of Pennsylvania excavation of Tikal, Tania and many of the staff worked three more years to finalize the massive Mayapán project. In spite of the tensions, these were productive years. The project provided field experience for a number of graduate students, including Bob Temple, Ann Chowning, and Donald Thompson, all of whom went on to successful careers. In her diary, Tania referred to Chowning and Thompson as "the kids," and under her supervision they excavated and drew up the plans for one of the outlying ceremonial groups at Mayapán.

In interviews with Chowning and Thompson,[97] both stated that Tania was treated as an equal in the heated discussions that took place among "the elders," as Chowning referred to them. Neither realized that by this time Tania and Ruppert, her friend of long standing, were not on speaking terms, a break that deeply saddened Tania.[98] Chowning, who shared a room with Tania for part of the season, had a unique perspective. She said that Tania went out each day to the ruins "looking impeccable in white jodhpurs" and rarely appeared dirty at the end of the day. She also said that "quarrels surfaced as the season wore on" and that Tania confided to her that she felt harassed by one of her colleagues. This claim indicates the degree of frustration Tania felt during much of the season.

Once back in Cambridge, Tania worked with the material on Mayapán. She had already written an article, "Mayapan: The Last Stronghold of a Civilization," that was published in 1954 in *Archaeology*. Two years later her article "The Death of a Civilization" appeared in *Scientific American*. The final publication on Mayapán came out in 1962. Edited by Pollock, it was titled *Mayapán, Yucatán, Mexico*, with Tania, Smith, and Roys as contributing authors.

Over the years numerous scholars have written about the demise of the Carnegie Institution's Department of Archaeology.[99] From their work as well as Tania's diary entries, it is clear that the cohesion and camaraderie of the earlier years were never regained after the hiatus necessitated by World War II. That the final years were marked at times by divisiveness and dissatisfaction does not reflect on the body of information and materials produced by this dynamic group of archaeologists over a span of half a century. It was with the aid and support of the Carnegie Institution for twenty of those years that Tania developed and honed the skills with which she would one day alter the direction of Maya studies. While this marked the end of an era for Mesoamerican archaeology, for Tania it was the beginning of a new period of reflection and self-discovery.

CHAPTER NINE

Resolution and Changing Priorities (1954–1958)

The demise of the Carnegie Institution of Washington's Department of Archaeology was a tumultuous event in the lives of its staff. Kidder had shouldered the bulk of the responsibility before retiring as its director, and he continued to feel burdened by its "failure" into the last years of his life.[1] Concerned and anxious, Pollock assumed Kidder's duties. Even for a man as thorough and conscientious as Pollock, the pressures were great and eventually took their toll, both physically and emotionally. It was in his role as director of the Department of Archaeology that he would deeply affect Tania's life.

Nine years Tania's senior, Harry Evelyn Dorr Pollock was born in Salt Lake City, Utah, on June 24, 1900.[2] When he was six months old, his mother died. His father, who worked as a mining engineer, decided to send the infant to Missouri to be raised by his aunts. At seven, the boy returned to live with his father and older brother, who now resided in California. He was later sent east to a respected college preparatory boarding school, the Hill School in Pottstown, Pennsylvania, where he participated on the winter track squad and, like Tania, was a member of the debate team. He was also active in the school's photography and gun clubs. As an undergraduate at Harvard University, Pollock joined the Fly Club. Harry graduated in 1923 with a major in literature and accepted a position with a brokerage firm in New York City. It was a job he disliked but remained with for the next few years. In 1927, over dinner at the Harvard Club, he listened as Ledyard Smith regaled him with exciting stories of his first field season on an archaeological dig in a remote region of Guatemala. Smith told him he thought there was work available the next year, if he wanted to leave his Wall Street job. As Willey noted, "This seemingly casual offer must have presented him with a very agonizing decision. . . . That he opted for archaeology, besides being a testament to his dislike of watching the ticker tape, tells us something of the inner romanticism which burned beneath that very proper and formal Pollock exterior."[3]

Ricketson, an older member of the Fly Club, hired Pollock to join his team at Uaxactún in 1928. Like others entering the field at this time, Pollock received his training in archaeological techniques on site. Between field seasons, he studied anthropology and archaeology under Alfred Tozzer at Harvard. Organized and disciplined, Pollock wrote a dissertation on round structures, such as the Caracol at Chichén Itzá, and received a Ph.D. in 1936. Pollock's field seasons were devoted to the study of Lowland Maya architecture and to the exploration of the recently discovered site of Cobá in Quintana Roo. The latter resulted in a joint publication with J. Eric S. Thompson and Jean Charlot. In 1937 Pollock, Shook, and Smith made their rugged reconnaissance trip through the Petén. Stopping at Piedras Negras, they related stories of their new discoveries and inspected the ruins with Satterthwaite and his team.[4] It was here that Pollock and Tania first met, though their careers would bring them together frequently in the years ahead.

When Pollock became director of the Department of Archaeology in 1950, he officially became the "boss" to friends and associates he had worked with for many years. Some had seniority over him at the Carnegie. It cannot have been an easy transition, but in his years as director, he proved an able leader. Tall, lean, and stately in appearance, he commanded respect from his colleagues and from the Maya who worked for him. He rarely raised his voice or used harsh words, for according to Willey, "he seemed to radiate a quiet authority."[5] This calm exterior, however, covered deep anxieties about the Carnegie's archaeological program, and he began to have problems with stomach ulcers. As the pressures built, Pollock increasingly relied on his closest colleagues. One of these was Tania.

There were many reasons that these two strong personalities were drawn to each other. Both had established a reputation for their work on Maya architecture, and both were highly intelligent, articulate, and well read. Their conversations ranged from light office gossip to cybernetics, carbon-14 dating, and literature. Both loved the works of Joseph Conrad, whose themes of adventure and the effects of primitive surroundings on human nature touched them. Tania observed, "[Conrad's] talent for writing is remarkable—unique. I know no one else who brings a situation into such strong focus."[6] Pollock enjoyed describing to his friends his first sleepless night as he traveled to the interior of Central America in a hammock slung between the poles of the boat's deck as "something out of Conrad."[7]

Tania and Pollock were both strong-willed and dedicated to their work. Ultimately, however, it was their work that kept them together, both in the Carnegie office and in the field. Early in her career, Tania noted in her diary that she felt agitated whenever he was around. On one occasion Pollock pointed out several mistakes she had made in her reconstruction drawing of Sayil, and, still in a temporary position as drafter, Tania was embarrassed and irritated by her carelessness. But there was more to her agitation. She had been to dinner with Pollock and enjoyed his company, and when he later announced his engagement to Katherine Winslow, a young woman from a prominent Boston family, Tania was disturbed. She wrote, "Although I have been expecting it, Harry's announcement that he is going to be married came as a shock, and I am afraid I was rather rude and didn't show much enthusiasm. I am, after all, fond of Harry—but I don't know just what my feelings are. If I do not want him but want him to want me—that's rather sordid. . . . I do hope he has chosen well."[8] In 1942 Pollock told his colleagues at the office that his wife was pregnant.[9] He soon left for Florida, where he trained with the U.S. Army Air Corps. After the war he

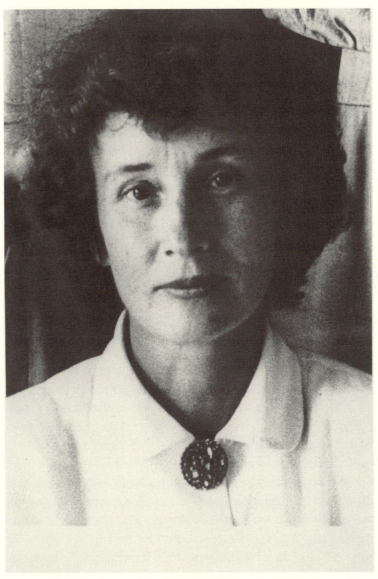

A closeup of Tania, taken from the CIW staff photo, Mayapán, 1952. Courtesy President & Fellows of Harvard College, Peabody, Museum, Harvard University (34821).

returned home to his wife and young son and resumed his work with CIW. Soon after, Kidder named Pollock his successor.

By 1951 the pressures of directing a doomed department were building for Pollock, and he often had discussions about this with Tania over lunch at the Faculty Club or at a nearby restaurant. Their relationship intensified. They began the season traveling together by train to New Orleans, then flying to Mérida. At Mayapán they worked closely together each day at the ruins. Stimulated by her agile mind, Pollock affectionately gave her the nickname "Plato." When Tania received word of her mother's brain tumor, she flew to Oregon. After her return to Yucatán, Pollock decided that they should go to Chichén Itzá to assess the photographic record of the sculpture there. It was an emotionally vulnerable time, and Tania, reflecting on this at the end of the field season, wrote, "The week in Chichén only makes everything worse. . . . I am calling myself every sort of fool . . . and I am somewhat surprised that the stupidity of my conduct doesn't greatly disturb me." Later she wrote, "I never got that walk around the block with Ed which I thought might ease my soul."[10] This marked the beginning of a tumultuous period in her relationship with Pollock.

The two wrestled for several years with the difficulty of their emotions. Pollock showed his affection by arriving unexpectedly at Tania's apartment door with armfuls of orange blossoms or taking her to New Hampshire for picnics on the bank of a river. Although his attentions were flattering, Tania wondered if Pollock's feelings for her could be "a slight aberration of approaching age" (he was in his early fifties).[11] She did not like the brusque way Pollock spoke to his wife on the telephone, and the sight of Katie dutifully running errands for her family saddened Tania. It was wrenching, and she felt these issues could not be resolved: "We came to a show down. I regret to say there have been several. I hope this is the last. Somehow it seems unfair that there is no honorable solution to the situation which doesn't do violence to one's feelings. I would much rather be kind."[12] Later she added, "I suppose it is inevitable that I can't take emotional disturbances more casually. I always seem to say the wrong things."[13] While she could talk with him about intellectual matters or details concerning their work, Tania was not comfortable expressing her emotions. This was in part because she was ambivalent. But finally she concluded, "I don't know why I can't just talk to him—it is so clear that there can't be anything between us. . . . Harry's problem of passion is not mine. . . . I cannot love him if I do not love him, however much I have suffered the same pangs myself. It is too late for that sort of thing."[14] In spite of this seeming realization, their complex relationship remained unresolved for several more years.

Tania's ongoing friendship with Strömsvik provided a balance to her intense relationship with Pollock. Describing a tender conversation with him, she wrote, "We talked of Harry's and Gus' feelings, too, which made me very sad. For what is this restless hankering for civilization that has kept me aloof all my life from foolish entanglements?"[15] Strömsvik remained at the Carnegie headquarters in Telchaquillo during the rainy seasons in 1954 and 1955, when the rest of the staff returned to Cambridge. He wrote warm letters to Tania, informing her of the latest village gossip and inquiring about the maneuverings of those in power at the Carnegie. Strömsvik retired the next year, ending a thirty-year career in Mesoamerican archaeology. From his home in Norway, where he built a sailboat large enough to sail to the Mediterranean each winter, he wrote Tania that he sometimes felt "more like a weather-tossed old derelict than a quasi, semi demi archaeologist retired."[16] In the coming years, she would deeply miss his stories, companionship, and affection. She wrote, "I shall miss him more than any friend I ever lost."[17]

Pollock's marriage survived this troubled time. He was also able to maintain a relationship with Tania on a professional level through the final tense years of the department, although it was significantly cooler. There were times when Tania longed to find work elsewhere. She remained out of loyalty to the department and to the people who had supported her career. Her loyalty was rewarded when Kidder convinced the CIW to keep Tania and two other staff members after the dissolution of the department.[18]

Tania entered a period of introspection during which she reevaluated her need for people. She wrote, "For the first time, I spent New Year [1954] alone, with no celebration, sitting in front of the fire and enjoying a book of crime stories."[19] She had recently moved into an apartment on one side of a nineteenth-century building, within walking distance of Harvard Square. It would be her home for the next thirty years. Her apartment on the ground floor had a bedroom, a kitchenette, and a study that opened into a dining room. From here, she had a view of the backyard garden.[20] Her landlady, Martha Taylor, lived upstairs, and though Tania at first feared that Taylor's "Cambridge background was a little formidable,"[21] the two women became loyal friends.

Taylor, schooled at home by her mother and physician father, overcame severe dyslexia as a child. After graduating from Radcliffe College in 1918, she became an editor of medical research reports and textbooks. While working on one of these texts, she "became convinced that conventional methods of dealing with young children were wrong."[22] After studying psychology at Columbia University, she returned to Cambridge and opened the Shady Hill School, which gained recognition for its high degree of success with difficult students. She later returned to her career in editing. Taylor was an intelligent, strong, professional woman, and she found in Tania a good friend. In the warmer months, the two often unwound from their workday, talking quietly together over drinks in the garden.

In the late 1950s, Tania turned increasingly to her women friends. They were a varied group. Some, such as Ginny Shook, Jo McCall, and Peggy Satterthwaite, were homemakers and happily married. Others were career women with whom she shared stimulating conversations about art, books, and politics. Among these friends were Cora Du Bois, a cultural anthropologist who in 1954 became the first tenured woman in the Department of Anthropology at Harvard,[23] and Suzanna Miles, an enthnohistorian who spent field seasons in the highlands of Guatemala. There were other friends, such as Suzanna's cousin, Heath Jones, Ruth Herndon, and the women Tania referred to as "the two Jeans," Jeane Murphy and Jean Taylor. Murphy and Taylor often invited her to join them for a weekend in Plymouth, where they relaxed with walks, conversations, and card games.[24]

Tania's niece, Norma Jean Ragsdale, explained in several interviews that some of Tania's friends were lesbians. Ragsdale related that one night one of these women had come to Tania's apartment, drunk and distraught, asking if Tania would become her lover. Tania declined but remained a close friend for many years. Tania's sister Kay told Ragsdale that she thought Tania was "asexual." Sexuality was perhaps less important for Tania than intellectual connection. She was nevertheless physically attracted to numerous men in her life, though she never experienced the mutual commitment needed to sustain a lifelong relationship. Her timing was perhaps poor, and her standards no doubt high. However, it may all come down to the explanation that Tania gave Ragsdale when she asked why Tania had never married: "Oh, dear, I was *much* to selfish for that!"[25] As she became older, her friendships with women, continued to sustain her. All shared a compassionate spirit and a quick mind. After Peggy Satterthwaite had visited Tania she wrote that she "was much impressed by the quality of the conversation" in her "salón" in Cambridge.[26]

Tania frequently also found comfort with the families of her friends, such as the McCalls in New York City and the Shooks outside of Boston. In the early 1950s Ed and Ginny had moved their three boys from Guatemala City and bought a house not far from that of Eric Thompson in Harvard. Tania frequently drove out on weekends, spending time with Ginny and taking long strolls in the countryside accompanied by the Shooks' youngest son. Now a retired navy captain living in North Carolina, John warmly recalled these walks. He said she encouraged him to take along his sketch pad so they could sit and sketch what they saw.[27] The way in which Tania shared her knowledge and love of drawing was much as her aunt Mila had done for her years before in Pennsylvania.

At times Tania invited her friends to vacation with her at her rustic retreat on Lake Winnepesaukee, a four-hour drive north of Boston. Over the years Avenir and Alla had often taken friends and family to enjoy the tranquillity and simple beauty of the place, and Tania carried on this tradition. She often sketched or painted on the porch overlooking the water while a friend lounged in the hammock slung between two pine trees. They swam, took the boat out on the lake for fishing, enjoyed long walks, and sometimes chopped firewood. Mostly they relaxed. On one

Tania drawing on the porch of her camp on Bear Island, Lake Winnepesaukee, New Hampshire, 1948. Courtesy of Mike Beetem.

trip, when she and friends had escaped a bad heat wave in the city, Tania
described "the beauty of a calm sunrise on the water" and continued,
"The loons were gay in the evening and laughing in their crazy way
somewhere very nearby. And the air smelled of pine needles after a
recent rain."[28]

Tania also made the trip alone, for she was increasingly in need of
solitude. She found that some of her friends' needs were becoming difficult to balance with her own: "The visits were too concentrated. I feel
as if I had forgotten what I was about, and I want to get back to an ordered
existence."[29] Later she added, "It is quite impossible today, it seems, to

Tania fishing at Champotón, Mexico. Courtesy of Dr. Edwin M. Shook.

go through the mere process of living without nervous strain; and to find time for meditation, reading and study is a dream."[30]

As one friend's eyesight began to fail, Tania went regularly to cook for her, staying to talk, but it was not enough. Tania described the woman's predicament, which was similar to what she would one day face: "Her struggle to preserve her independence is hard to cope with, for she resents both sympathy and indifference and will not admit that being alone is not safe for her. . . . There is something quite impressive in her determination to assert her status."[31]

Tania's tendency to take contrary positions began to take its toll on some of her friendships. After one incident, she wrote,

> The reaction one sometimes gets from a simple remark that doesn't happen to accord with their concept of how a conversation should go is so out of proportion. . . . Both women in conversation invite only confirmation and I usually give it to them— only occasionally not. However, they seem to be the wrong occasions. . . . The fault was a critical remark I made of a final explanatory statement in her little story . . . but the result was apparently brutal—a poetic attitude is fragile.[32]

Numerous associates concurred with Ian Graham when he described Tania's "propensity for lightly but almost automatically contradicting her colleagues, a habit that most of them regarded more with amused indulgence than irritation."[33] For her friends, however, Tania's criticisms appear to have been more difficult to swallow.

Tania began to spend more time alone, a decision that would haunt her late in life. She once again turned to books for nourishment and inspiration. They were, as always, diverse and included Suzanne Langer's *Feeling and Form*, Pasternak's *Dr. Zhivago*, and various works by Freud, Cassire, and Montaigne. Reflecting on the impact of reading on her life, she wrote, "When I read good books, my writing does not exactly improve, but it becomes much easier."[34]

When the door finally closed on the offices of the CIW Department of Archaeology, Tania settled into her new basement office next door at the Peabody Museum of Archaeology and Ethnology, where she had been named Research Fellow in Maya Art. She wrote, "It seems like what I always wanted. . . . It is very satisfying to be doing research again instead of merely descriptive reports."[35] This marked the beginning of a period that Joyce Marcus described as the "most exciting" for Tania professionally.[36] The years ahead were indeed among her most productive.

CHAPTER TEN

Research, Hieroglyphs, and Further Adventure (1958–1965)

With her move to the Peabody Museum, Tania was now free to choose her own projects.[1] While she continued to gather and write "Mesoamerican Notes and News" for the quarterly journal *American Antiquity*, much of her time could now be devoted to research. This eventually led her back to one of her early interests and the subject of her first publication, the hieroglyphic inscriptions of Piedras Negras. Those texts became the primary focus of her powerful intellect.

In summer 1958 Tania made two new readings of dates on the monuments of Piedras Negras, noting, "The dynastic hypothesis is breaking down but something may yet be salvaged from the idea." She later wrote, "I have been working at home on stela groupings and date arrangements. Although no simple solution has emerged as yet, certain patterns are suggested that may have real significance."[2] As she continued to work with this material, her emotions were intense: "My mood alternates between elation with the results of my hypothesis and depression when I think I have inflated the whole thing."[3] Through her study of the location of the various stelae, coupled with meticulous scholarship, she was able to support her hypothesis. Her resulting twenty-one-page article,

"Historical Implications of a Pattern of Dates at Piedras Negras, Guatemala," was published in *American Antiquity* in 1960.

Refuting the view prevalent among many scholars of the time that Maya writing was astronomical or religious in nature, concerned primarily with the passage of time, Tania showed for the first time that the inscriptions at Piedras Negras almost certainly dealt with history. Through structural analysis of the texts, she identified glyphs for birth and accession, establishing when these important events took place in the lives of individual rulers. Tania was able to prove her "historical hypothesis" so logically that, as University of Arizona archaeologist Patrick Culbert writes, "not a single voice was raised in protest—unlike many scholarly revolutions that are argued bitterly for years before acceptance."[4]

Tania acknowledged that her breakthrough was possible because she built on the findings of earlier scholars, but she also relied on certain colleagues whose input challenged and stimulated her research, among them Maya studies' greatest scholars. Before the Piedras Negras article, Thompson believed it was inconceivable that the glyphic texts contained written records of events and deeds of individual rulers. Tania wrote him a letter about her findings before sending her paper to be published. From his home in Saffron Walden, England, he responded, "I was very glad to learn of your progress in the 'dynasty' research. It will upset a cherished theory of mine that the Maya were so superior to the rest of mankind that they kept themselves out of the stelae and forbore to record their wars, triumphs & extinctions! However, theories are made to be upset, & if you can, or, I should say, have cracked the problem, it will be a huge stride forward."[5] Several years later he revised the text of his *Rise and Fall of the Maya Civilization* to incorporate some of the dramatic changes that had occurred since its initial publication in 1954. He wrote to Tania, "I have been busy changing statements about the impersonality of the stelae texts. . . . Had you waited to make your discoveries until I had left this Vale of Tears, you would have saved me a lot of work, or had I the ability . . . to admit no mistake, I would also have avoided the toil & sweat & (contrite) tears."[6] Their correspondence over the next fifteen years was an open exchange of ideas, demonstrating a deep respect for each other's work.

Tania also regularly communicated with a friend and colleague who shared her interest in Maya hieroglyphs. The two had become acquainted during visits to Mexico City and during a period at Mayapán. This was Heinrich Berlin, who in 1935 escaped Nazi persecution and fled to Mexico, where he and his family started a wholesale grocery business. In 1940 Berlin began to work at the archaeological site of Palenque, where he became intrigued, as many had before him, by the hieroglyphic inscriptions there.[7]

Based on his years of glyph research, Berlin wrote many articles, the best known of which was published in 1958. In this article, he identified certain glyphs he called "Place Glyphs" or "Emblem Glyphs," which he found associated with specific sites. Referring to his next work, dealing with rulers' names, Tania wrote, "I received a paper on name glyphs from Berlin—his work ties in with mine completely and I am encouraged that we can work with monuments on a historical basis."[8] After reading a draft of a paper she had sent to him, he responded, "I think there can be no doubt about the existence of the system which you discovered."[9] Frustrated that Tania's article was not scheduled to be published for another year, Berlin wrote, "It is a shame that such a paper will have to remain unpublished for so long a time. . . . Isn't there any other suitable place where it could come out earlier?"[10] He continued with questions for Tania: "Apparently you have no clear-cut dates for the death of the different rulers, which we would expect to find inscribed prominently. Will you do me the favor and look for them and get them!?!"[11] She followed through and found the dates. Over the next twenty years, Tania and Berlin kept up their lively correspondence and on several occasions had the opportunity to meet and talk. They kept each other informed of new directions in their research, exchanged interpretations of glyphs, and found challenge and support in their friendship.

Tania also maintained a steady correspondence with Satterthwaite, the bulk of the letters dealing with the dating of monuments, using the charts she had put together for this purpose in *A Study of Classic Maya Sculpture*. In one letter Satterthwaite responded to a note from Tania: "As usual your insights are always profound and provocative."[12] Their correspondence stimulated new ideas, and in a reply to Satterthwaite, Tania wrote,

> I wonder . . . whether we fundamentally disagree on what the ancient Maya did achieve. . . . [Y]ou suggest that cities were 'religious' or 'priest-built.' . . . I don't doubt that the priesthood was politically important . . . but what I'd like to stress is that there was an intelligentsia—a group of artists and scholars and 'master-builders.' . . . I'm sure the sculptor who carved a great period stela was only incidentally interested in its religious significance and centered his attention on the graceful curves of feathers and the modeling of the human form, and other such universally interesting truths.[13]

In 1959 she sent him a draft of her Piedras Negras article for his suggestions. He responded, "I haven't any worth-while criticism of the theoretical part of the paper. It's the most reasonable explanation for a non-cyclical as well as a non-astronomical pattern. I take that now as demonstrated. Congratulations on a brilliant job."[14]

The relationship between Tania and David H. Kelley also proved important to the future of Maya hieroglyphic decipherment. Kelley, who had come to Harvard on the GI Bill after serving in the army in WWII, was one of Alfred Tozzer's last students and among Gordon Willey's first. While studying in the late 1940s and the 1950s at the Peabody Museum, he found Tania readily accessible to him at the CIW and later at the Peabody. In an interview Kelley said that Tania was easy to talk with about his ideas concerning the Maya writing system and that a relationship developed between them that was both argumentative and respectful.[15] This is borne out in the tone of their frequent correspondence.

Kelley, who was also in regular contact with Satterthwaite, was working on a phonetic approach to glyph analysis that had been suggested by the Russian linguist Yuri Knorosov. At the time it was a daring direction for an American Mayanist to pursue. In the tense atmosphere of the cold war, there was powerful resistance to *any* Russian's ideas. Not one to back down from controversy, Tania translated one of Knorosov's articles in 1953. A short time later, Satterthwaite wrote to ask, "Is there any chance of having your translation copied or photo-stated for our use down here? Our Russian expert . . . would undertake its translation but I don't see any sense in duplicating yours."[16] In 1957 she mentioned in her diary, "Most of my day was taken up by . . . translating Knorosov's latest article for Dave Kelley."[17] Tania did not find this linguistic approach productive for her own work, and she died before many of the glyph readings based on it were made. However, she encouraged Kelley in his pursuit, writing in a letter, "I'm awfully glad you are taking this up."[18] She also cautioned him: "[I] hope you can get some good demonstrable values." She noted in her diary that he had "dropped in one evening" and talked "about glyphs until 2:00 A.M."[19] This support for Kelley and her later work as editor of Sophie Coe's translations of selected chapters from Knorosov's *Writing of the Maya Indians*, show that Tania believed it was important to make the Russian scholar's papers accessible to Western researchers.

The content of the hieroglyphic inscriptions from another major Maya site on the Usumacinta, fifty kilometers upriver from Piedras Negras, also attracted Tania's attention. By analyzing the inscribed stone lintels from Yaxchilán, she established a dynastic sequence for the site. The Boston University art historian Clemency Coggins writes that "the Piedras Negras and Yaxchilán inscriptions recorded different kinds of historical information from each other, on different kinds of monuments."[20] In spite of this, Tania was able to accurately name the rulers, rather than refer to them by number as she had in the Piedras Negras paper, and to reconstruct the history of the Jaguar dynasty from the eighth century A.D. The two-part article based on her research was titled "Historical Data in the Inscriptions of Yaxchilán" and appeared in the journal *Estudios de Cultura Maya*. This was the first in a long series of papers by various scholars that have since explored the dynastic sequence of the major Classic Period cities of the Maya.

Tania next chose to write a piece for the general public in which she explained the steps she went through to arrive at her historical hypothesis. Appearing in *Expedition Magazine*, "The Lords of the Maya Realm" opens,

We Mayanists spend an inordinate amount of time deciphering half obliterated hieroglyphic texts. Often it seems that our results are not worth all that effort; but now and again some minor fact that hardly seems worth mentioning at the time can be used to pry open a chink in the wall of obscurity that surrounds the past, and suddenly we get a new and exciting glimpse of events that have left their traces on the old stones of Maya sites.[21]

The combined effect of Tania's articles was stunning. They solidified her reputation for thorough and meticulous scholarship and pointed Maya scholars in important new directions. In 1990 Jeremy Sabloff, director of the University of Pennsylvania Museum, noted that after their publication, "[o]ther scholars set off to look for similar inscriptions elsewhere with spectacular success." He continued, "Coggins . . . was actually able to work out a kinship chart tracing the generations of rulers from the time of the founder of the Tikal 'dynasty' through much of the Classic period. She was also able to link some of the rulers with particular tombs. Moreover, she and others were able to show that the texts talked about marriage alliances and relations between centers."[22] Since then, decipherment of the existing texts has rapidly escalated. According to David Stuart, a leading Maya epigrapher, "Today, about 80 percent of Maya inscriptions are readable, and the writing system is essentially deciphered."[23] These texts focus on royalty and nobles, not on the daily lives of commoners, but as modern archaeologists gather and analyze new material, a more complete picture of Maya civilization will emerge. In the early 1960s Tania pointed the way.

Tania made another contribution at this time when she prepared a chapter for the book being put together to honor the archaeologist Samuel K. Lothrop. She chose as her topic the depictions of women in Maya art, a view that, while suggested by several earlier scholars, did not have wide acceptance at the time. Most notable archaeologists of the time believed that the figures appearing in robes on the monuments were priests, and this premise was little questioned.[24] Once again Tania moved cautiously. She wrote, "I worked on Lothrop's festschrift— women on Maya monuments, but I am not sure I am entirely convinced of what I write."[25] However, as she worked through the evidence she became increasingly confident in her results. One of her former students, David Freidel of Southern Methodist University, wrote, "Tania believed that one should not publish an argument concerning Maya art, even in article form, until it was incontrovertibly proven."[26] Although it required great self-discipline, her strict adherence to such principles has kept her work at the forefront of Maya studies in the years since her death. In "Portraits of Women in Maya Art," Tania again presented new evidence, this time by identifying the glyphs associated with women. In 1995 Marcus wrote, "Thanks to her, we now know that the robed figures considered to be priests by Morley and Thompson were in fact royal women."[27]

While working on these pathbreaking articles, Tania also made several trips to Mexico. In 1959 she flew to Mexico City. She would have preferred traveling by train, "[b]ut trains are almost twice as expensive and one must inure oneself to the madness of one's age."[28] A day later she flew to Tuxtla Gutiérrez in the southern state of Chiapas, where she had been asked to assist with a ceramics collection at a new anthropological museum. A delegation of teachers came to meet her, and the local newspaper published an article on her. In her diary she fretted that the reporter described her as an "Artista Polaca," a Polish Artist, causing her to write, "Where they got the idea I can't imagine."[29] Working at the museum with Bruce Warren and Berlin, she enjoyed the leisurely pace and lack of fuss. Warren occasionally invited Tania to have dinner with his wife and children. At their request, she went with them to the Mormon Sunday service, which seemed to her "inexpressibly dreary," though she read the *Book of Mormon*, finding it to be "rather good."[30] She also made trips into the countryside, where she was entranced by the Cañón del Sumidero: "Such magnificence! A deep gorge with the river far below—looking almost motionless. . . . Green slopes rise to sheer white and red cliffs with clouds dropping and rising and mist racing along the cut. . . . I have seen it in Honduras and Guatemala, but El Sumidero is one of the best."[31]

It was during her stay in Tuxtla that she had the opportunity to meet Bobbie Montagu, a colorful American woman who had made her home in nearby San Cristóbal de las Casas. Tania described her as "a charming young woman[,] . . . marvelously mysterious to me, a wonder. And so friendly to a stranger."[32] Montagu invited Tania to visit with her in her home, which she soon did. Writing about the "wonderful weekend" she spent there, she described the home as "a big neglected house with patios overgrown with weeds, a bathroom that has a shower but no wash basin . . . There is a kitchen a block away to which one tramps on cold flagstones wet with dew in the morning[,] . . . also, a Great Dane, an Afghan hound and a mutt, a parrot, a macaw, and two cats."[33] Completing this unusual household was an adopted Maya child named Tete, who later moved to Cuba, where she was trained in classical ballet.

Famous for her colorful tales,[34] Montagu said that she had met her late husband, Lord Montagu, during World War II, when she disguised herself as a man in order to serve as a sailor onboard a naval ship. They later married and traveled together to Mexico. When her husband died suspiciously from a fall during an ill-equipped expedition into the rugged backcountry of the Mexican highlands, Montagu remained in San Cristóbal. Her home eventually became headquarters for Harvard anthropologist Evon Z. Vogt's Chiapas Project, an extensive, long-term study of the modern Highland Maya. At the time of Tania's visit, Montagu's home was already a place where anthropologists and archaeologists regularly gathered, and she enjoyed the atmosphere: "It makes me feel very much alive to be in a world that doesn't cater to one's habitual demands."[35] She entertained the idea of someday relocating to San Cristóbal. Though Tania later changed her mind, Montagu wrote in an undated letter to her, "Remember, I am keeping a lot for you at the new colonia for when you find New Hampshire too crowded."[36]

Tania enjoyed their far-ranging conversations as well as Montagu's extensive library. Describing her new friend as an "avid reader" who "knows more about what goes on at home than we do,"[37] Tania later sent her copies of her books. In an exchange with Brigham Young University, she also sent copies of their publications dealing with the archaeology of Chiapas. After Montagu's death, this library was donated to the research center, Na Bolom, the former home of the archaeologist Frans Blom and his wife, Trudi.[38]

In letters to Tania, Montagu described the setting for her fieldwork in remote Bachajón: "It is rugged. There are no roads . . . so everything must be packed in . . . to the great center . . . where there are only 10 or 12 houses and the people live out on little ranches. . . . It is all simply dreamy and I am working hard to learn Tzeltal." Montagu was asked to contribute a piece on the Tojolabal Indians to the *Handbook of Middle American Indians*. Concerned that "[e]verybody else will be terribly scholarly," she wrote, "I am not really an ethnographer but rather a frustrated Girl Scout."[39]

While in Mexico in 1962, Tania again spent some time in San Cristóbal. She was en route to Guatemala City to do some work for Kidder at Kaminaljuyu, and Montagu offered to drive her there. Along with Montagu's friend, Sonia Pitt-Rivers, once the wife of George Orwell, the three women drove in a Land Rover across the border into the highlands of Guatemala. They took their time, stopping in many villages along the way. While noting in her diary that she felt friction with Rivers, Tania described the time in a letter to her sister as a "magnificent trip, with gorges and mountains and hair-pin turns all the way."[40] It was the last time Tania and Montagu saw each other. Later that year, receiving word of Montagu's unexpected death, she wrote simply of her friend, "I have seldom met anyone I have liked so much."[41]

Earlier in 1962 Tania had stayed in Mexico City for several months, working at the museum on their collection of Jaina figurines. It was a social time. She enjoyed dinners at the home of Alberto Ruz or with her friends Heinrich Berlin and Carmen Cook. With Cook, she took a bus south to Cuernavaca, where they met Ruz and his wife for a visit to the excavation at Xochicalco. Together they attended a dance and met the new Mexican Labor leader, who was among the guests. Tania wrote, "What impressed me most was the immense gulf between Indian and Mexican and the distrust and lack of communication between them."[42]

Her visit to Guatemala City later in 1962, however, was tense. As she wrote to her sister, "The curfew and martial law that was imposed when the Chief of Police was killed has been lifted, but there are still student demonstrations and protests of all kinds. . . . I hope they don't start shooting it out while I'm at the ruins. I'd hate to have to hole up in one of the tunnels." Drawing up plans of the excavation, which she had agreed to do for Kidder, turned out to be more work than she had anticipated, but, she said it was "a man-sized job . . . and I like it."[43] The ruins were a long bus ride to the opposite side of the city from the museum, and she felt she was wasting a great deal of time traveling back and forth. Because the demonstrations had caused many businesses to close, she could not get the equipment she needed and rigged up her own handmade level to use in surveying. This was a minor inconvenience compared to what was to come: "My first intimation of trouble was when I was returning from the ruins, and the streets were reeking of teargas. . . . There are sporadic outbreaks all over town. . . . No one seems to know how serious the trouble is apt to be. . . . I'd planned to fly to Tikal for a few days, but am tempted to skip it." The next day she wrote, "The city seems ominously quiet. There is no one on the streets. Jeeps full of soldiers are patrolling." And then: "Aside from a hold up of some buses with machine guns and the killing of a drunk who threw a bottle at some soldiers, nothing has happened . . . and I am back working at the ruins."

In spite of her fears about flying into the jungle, Tania visited the University of Pennsylvania excavation at Tikal. This massive archaeological project was begun in 1955, under Shook's direction. Located in the lush Petén rain forest, Tikal was one of the greatest centers of the Classic Maya, an exciting choice for a multidisciplinary project. Over the years it has yielded vast amounts of information on the Maya. The beauty of the natural setting and the magnificent architecture of Tikal combine to make it a popular destination for travelers in Central America, and it has become the centerpiece of the hugely successful Guatemalan tourism business. In the years since the project's inception, the area surrounding the ruins has become a national park and wildlife refuge, where large numbers of animals, including spider and howler monkeys, are protected.[44] Tania's visit there was was a happy one.

She spent several days looking over the ruins. Robert Dyson, Tikal director, later wrote to her, "I have been meaning to write a thank-you note on behalf of the staff for your generous contribution to our off-hours enjoyment. . . . It was great fun having you here and your visit was a high point in our season for everyone."[45] In an interview, Culbert, who was among those present during her visit, remembered that one evening the archaeologists and graduate students gathered to unwind from the day's work. Free from the tensions in Guatemala City, Tania joined in, dancing the Twist around the campfire.[46] She wrote, "It was really fun to see the jungle again, and the great pyramids are certainly impressive, so I am very glad I went."[47]

Happily, this was not Tania's last time in the Petén. In 1965 Willey and Smith asked her to visit the sites of Seibal and Altar de Sacrificios, where they were conducting excavations for the Peabody Museum. To make the trip, Tania had to fly in a small plane to the remote village of Sayaxché, where a narrow dirt landing strip had been cleared from the surrounding jungle. In an interview, Willey related that on hearing the sound of an approaching airplane, the villagers would rush to clear the runway of chickens and pigs. From here, he said Tania traveled down the Pasión River for eight hours in a dugout canoe powered by a small outboard motor.[48] Altar de Sacrificios, at the confluence of two rivers, is on low, swampy ground. Shook described that the site was swarming with so many mosquitoes he believed they "had originated there and then spread to the rest of the world."[49]

Seibal was a more pleasant site to visit for Tania. Two hours upriver from Sayaxché, it is situated high on a bluff overlooking the Pasión. While there, she was put up in a simple, thatched guest house. Working only with fragments found on and around the structure, Tania made a reconstruction drawing of the stucco frieze on Structure A-III. Her drawing, later included in Smith's report on the project, *Architecture, Burials and Caches of Seibal*, required talent, patience, and great skill to deduce so much from so few scattered remains.

It was at Sayaxché that Tania first met Ian Graham, one of the more dynamic personalities among today's active Mayanists, a man who would become increasingly important to her in the years ahead. She described him as "an interesting chap and an A-1 explorer."[50] Graham, the grandson of a Scottish duke, was in the early stages of his productive career, having discovered his great passion for the carved hieroglyphic inscriptions of the Classic Maya while in his thirties.[51] Their meeting at Sayaxché would have far-reaching effects for both Graham and Tania, as well as for the future of Maya scholarship.

Tania made only two other trips back to Central America in the coming years, both of which gave her spirits "a lift."[52] She now became increasingly involved with a project at the Peabody Museum—restoring and cataloging the carved jades that had been dredged, early in the century, from the Sacred Cenote at Chichén. This project, coupled with the opportunity to work with a dynamic group of students, kept her busy for the next twenty years.

CHAPTER ELEVEN

Seminars, Jades, and Accolades (1965–1985)

During the 1960s and 1970s, as Tania settled into the routine of work in her basement office at the Peabody Museum, an increasing number of students turned to her for advice and guidance. Many of them recalled that she would frequently head down the hall from her office to the Smoking Room to enjoy a cigarette. Although it was a dark, basement room, this was the only place in the museum where smoking was permitted, and so it was a natural gathering place for museum associates and students as well. Sitting on an odd assortment of chairs and seats, which had originally been part of a design project, the colleagues who frequently joined Tania were Gordon Willey, Evon Vogt, and Ledyard and Robert Smith. Their conversations were colorful and varied, and the sociable atmosphere made them want to linger.

One of the students who often was present during the 1970s was Linnea Wren, now an art historian at Gustavus Adolphus College. While an undergraduate at Radcliffe, she had taken several art courses at Harvard in which Tania invited students to make use of the sculpture and photographic files in her office. She recalls, "Tania was never effusive, but she was gently accepting. . . . She never imposed any ideas on me but was always encouraging. And she would stress the prime importance of looking at Maya art."[1] Wren, whose father was a professor at Yale University, was comfortable in this environment and, along with others like David Freidel, appreciated the intellectual exchanges that took place. Earlier, students had included Jeremy Sabloff, Joyce Marcus, and Clemency Coggins, all now prominent scholars in their fields. Often their discussions with Tania would continue over lunch at a Chinese restaurant in Harvard Square or dinner at her nearby apartment. Each acknowledges that Tania gave generously of her time and energy.

Tania also made a deep and lasting impression on Richard Townsend, curator of the Department of African and Amerindian Art at the Chicago Art Institute. He states,

> Tania was very gracious, receiving me in the basement of the Peabody. She was unassuming and encouraging. . . . Few people in the world of archaeology at this time understood the religious basis of these ancient cultures. . . . Her studies led her to the notion of an animistic world in which the gods of the various Mesoamerican cultures were related but never with human personalities, like Hera or Zeus. They are rather manifestations of the forces of nature, the mountains, the rain, and the lightning, never attaining anthropomorphism. She alluded to this in a gentle fashion.

Townsend also notes that Tania "had a quiet way of passing on this vision. . . . [T]o talk with Tania was also to be gently reminded that a scholar's purpose is best served by avoiding an excess of public or administrative life."[2]

Avoidance of public life was becoming increasingly difficult for Tania as she became more recognized for her contributions in the field. In 1962 it was announced that she would be the recipient of the Alfred Vincent Kidder Award for Eminence in the Field of American Archaeology. She was presented the very medal she had designed twelve years earlier. That summer, in a letter to Tania, Satterthwaite wrote, "Three cheers and then some for you. I hear via Eric [Thompson] in England that you have the Kidder medal. . . . He said in effect that you were the biggest thing in Maya studies in the last twenty years. About that there

Tania, undated. Courtesy of Mike Beetem.

can be no doubt. . . . Anyway, I'm tickled to death. It reminds me again of one time you looked at me darkly and opined that no woman could get a square deal in this field."[3] She was the first woman, and at this writing the only woman, to be so honored.

That same year she was asked to participate in an international symposium to be held at Burg Wartenstein, Austria. Sponsored by the Wenner-Gren Foundation for Anthropological Research, Evon Z. Vogt organized the conference, "The Cultural Development of the Maya." Although international meetings are now a regular occurrence for Mayanists, the Wartenstein symposium was the first time eminent scholars from around the world came together to deal with the question of Maya linguistics and social structure. Besides Vogt and Tania, the scholars who were invited to attend included Alberto Ruz, Sol Tax, Alfonso Rojas, Henning Siverts, Thomas Barthel, Gunter Zimmermann, Gordon R. Willey, Wolfgang Haberland, and Munro Edmonson.[4] Yuri Knorosov, the Russian linguist whose work Tania had helped to make accessible to the West, was unable to attend. At this time the Soviet government still kept a tight rein on its scientists and scholars, and permission to travel out of the country was rare. A meeting between Tania and this important man would not take place for another eight years, when she made her only return visit to her homeland.

An automobile accident in her Volkswagen Bug earlier that summer of 1962 had left her on crutches for six weeks, but she was still able to prepare for her part in the conference. She wrote her sister from Cambridge, "With the Vienna trip in the offing, I'll be keeping my nose to the grindstone." When Kay sent her a check to use on her travels, Tania responded, "You overwhelm me. . . . It isn't money that keeps me away from touring Europe—it's *fame*! I got in this morning's mail: 1) a paper (manuscript) from a guy in Mexico on early Spanish accounts of Maya art and architecture[,] . . . 2) Three papers (50 pages each) I must read for the conference[,] . . . 3) A manuscript of 300 pages from Stanford University Press asking me to comment and tell them if they should publish it. And so it goes. In between times, I try to get some work done."[5]

After the end of the conference, from the comfort of her apartment, she wrote to Kay once again. She described "wandering around in a kind of daze trying to get back into the old routine—quite a change from the dream-castle, the snow-capped mountains, the wine and the conversation in several languages." She continued,

> We met for three hours each morning and two in the afternoon, but occasionally . . . we were taken for a jaunt—once to the vineyard near the Hungarian border, where we tasted all the wines and ended up singing Austrian, French, Mexican, Cowboy and even Russian songs. I learned quite a bit about linguistics and some about social organization of various Maya tribes. . . . It was much better than the enormous society meetings where one really never gets a chance to talk to anyone. We were only eleven.[6]

Papers presented at the conference were later edited by Vogt and Ruz and published in Mexico under the title *Desarrollo cultural de los Mayas*. Tania's paper, which Berlin translated into Spanish, was titled "El arte Maya y el modelo genético de cultura."[7]

Settled back in Cambridge, an invitation from the Worcester Art Museum in Massachusetts provided Tania with a creative diversion. The museum was preparing an exhibition of Maya architecture, having recently completed the renovation of their Pre-Columbian Gallery. Tania agreed to lend some of the original architectural reconstruction drawings she had made for her *Album*. Many of these same drawings and watercolors can now be seen in the Maya displays at the Peabody Museum of Harvard, while one, of Uaxactún, is displayed at the Museo Nacional de Guatemala, and the famous watercolor of the Acropolis of Piedras Negras is housed at the University of Pennsylvania Museum Archives. For the Worcester exhibition, her drawings were hung along with recent photographs of the ruins taken by the architect Norman Carver. The exhibition also featured a large, recently acquired carved column from the Mexican state of Campeche that required a reinforced floor, and on loan from Shook, twenty-five of Frederick Catherwood's hand-colored lithographs of the Maya ruins that had been published in folios in 1844.[8] Shook and Tania were invited to attend a cocktail party in their honor at the opening of the exhibition. In a letter to Kay, she worried over having to buy a new dress, an appropriate hat, and accessories for the occasion, but she was pleased that the museum suggested she invite ten of her close friends. She added, "This affair should be fun."[9]

Tania also continued her long-term jade project at the museum. Some of the tedious work on the jades involved reassembling broken pieces from the many fragments in the collection, and in her diary she wrote, "I was involved all day putting together a new jade—a strange creature I cannot identify yet."[10] For some of the fragments, she was able to supply details of the missing designs from her vast knowledge of Maya art. The result of more than ten years of work, *Jades from the Cenote of Sacrifice* was published in 1974. In it, Tania described the condition of the collection: "Very few pieces are even approximately complete, and the majority remained in disarticulated parts. In order to make the nature of their designs clear, it was necessary to reconstruct the missing portions. The size and range [of the collection] imbue it with a unique value for those who are seriously interested in the history of the lapidary arts of Mesoamerica or in the specific content of Maya culture."[11]

Two years after publication of the jade book, Stephen Williams, then director of the Peabody Museum, asked Tania to select pieces of the collection to present to Mexico. The American delegation included Williams; Derek Bok, president of Harvard University; and Eric von Euw, assistant to Ian Graham and Research Fellow in Maya Hieroglyphs at the Peabody. In a ceremony in Mexico City, the delegation presented the jades to Luis Echeverría, president of Mexico. A press release from the Harvard News Office states, "[T]he artifacts will be made part of the national collections in the country of their origin with the understanding that research materials will be made available to the Peabody . . . to aid in the teaching of Mexican archaeology."[12] For Tania, it was a gratifying end to a long, involved project. Soon thereafter, Berlin wrote to her, "To think that you devoted some 15 years of your life on it increases my admiration and respect beyond limits. Certainly somebody had to do the job sometime anyhow, but you made the actual sacrifice, which it must have been, despite the satisfaction to have written another everlasting contribution in the Maya field."[13]

While her work on the jades was still in progress, Tania was again invited to participate in a conference at Burg Wartenstein. Titled

Tania working on jades in her office at the Peabody Museum, 1974. Courtesy President & Fellows of Harvard College, Peabody Museum, Harvard University (N 31681).

"Emergent Civilization in Mesoamerica as Compared to parallel Developments in the Old World," it was held in July 1970 and included Claude Baudez, Anne Chapman, Ignacio Bernal, E. Wyllys Andrews, Ed Shook, John Graham, and George Kubler. Tania took notes on the papers delivered but for the most part was a quiet participant. She enjoyed her breaks from the meetings, sitting in the sun and making simple pencil sketches of the beautiful surroundings.[14] Accompanied by the younger anthropologist, Anne Chapman, with whom she had become friendly, she visited galleries in Vienna. She wrote that they saw "nothing exciting." "The past is present, but the present is drab."[15]

Tania had decided earlier that year that she would take the opportunity at the end of the conference to travel to Russia to meet with Yuri Knorosov at the Institute of Ethnology in Leningrad. Given the political atmosphere of the Soviet Union in the years before glasnost, such a trip was a challenge both logistically and emotionally. It was her first and only return visit to her homeland. Before leaving Cambridge, in a conversation with her friend, Phillippa Shaplin, she had expressed deep concerns about her ability to communicate fluently in her native tongue.[16] Although she had continued to read in Russian, as an adult she had little opportunity to speak the language. She proceeded, nevertheless, to make the necessary arrangements for this complicated leg of her trip.

Accompanied by a woman she referred to in her diary as "Olga," she flew from Vienna to Moscow and found the international airport in "utter chaos." After frustrating delays, which resulted in missing their reserved flight, they finally got seats on another flight. They arrived late at night in Leningrad and went directly to their hotel. The next day Tania went to see Knorosov's colleague, R. W. Kinjhalov, who had written a general text on Maya culture that was soon to be published, but she found only his assistant at the institute. Later both Kinjhalov and Knorosov, whom she described as a "strange pair," came to meet her at the hotel. From there, they took her on a tour of Petergof, the imperial palace built in the early eighteenth century by Peter the Great. Tania thought it was "spectacular" but was put off by the crowds.[17]

The following morning, Knorosov came again to talk with her about Maya glyphs, but their conversation was soon interrupted when Kinjhalov arrived unannounced. During this period, it would have been most unusual for Tania, a naturalized American citizen, to be allowed to speak alone with Knorosov. Typically, an additional person was always present, such as a translator or someone who reported to or was directly in the service of the KGB, the Soviet secret police. Under these circumstances, it is understandable that no further description of their meeting exists.[18] Tania's single diary entry about her days in Russia is quite short, and a search through Knorosov's archived papers by his assistant, Galina Yershova, was equally unfruitful. Yershova reported, however, that Tania's visit had been very important to Knorosov, as it occurred during a difficult period, when he was not permitted to leave Russia or to have outside contacts.[19] Knowing her family's ties to Czar Nicholas's Imperial Army, he clearly understood the risk she had taken in coming, and he viewed it almost as an "act of heroism" on her part. In conversations with Marcus shortly after her trip, she expressed some sadness at how little of what she saw in Russia corresponded with her childhood memories.[20] However, she never wrote or spoke about whether she looked for relatives while in Leningrad. It was here in the winter of 1916 that an uncle had provided rooms for her mother, sister, and her while the girls recovered sufficiently to continue their journey to join Avenir in America. Tania also never mentioned if she had wanted to travel to her family's home city of Tomsk, which was, in 1970, still strictly off-limits to foreigners. After three days, Tania and Olga traveled by train through Norway and Sweden, then took a steamer to Denmark before returning to the United States.[21]

Back in Cambridge, Tania began to worry about increasingly frequent memory lapses, weakening eyesight, unexplained headaches, and greater demands on her time. She wrote, "There seems to be more work than I can do but it is no longer pressing. . . . I am trying to cut down a little on smoking and exercise in the morning, but I am not trying very hard." She added, "Why do we live so hectically? . . . One would think a person living alone and in such a position of freedom as I could do what she likes—but the demands others make on me are exorbitant."[22]

Among other demands on Tania's time was an increased teaching load of courses on Maya art at Harvard University and elsewhere. She was invited to give a semester seminar at Columbia University but, not fond of New York City, she declined. However, she accepted an offer from Michael Coe to lecture at Yale. In fall 1977 Tania also received the honor of serving as Andrew W. Mellon Professor of Fine Arts at the University of Pittsburgh.[23] During this semester, she sublet her Cambridge apartment and moved into a place in the Shadyside district of Pittsburgh. Although her cousin, Andrew Chenzoff, who lived north of the city, visited her on several occasions,[24] socially it was a very different environment from her normal existence in Cambridge. She was in her sixties, living in an unfamiliar place, and giving a lecture course and a graduate seminar on Maya art. It was a challenging experience for her.

Tania often worried over public appearances and preferred the small seminars of approximately ten students she conducted with Willey at Harvard. These were described by Marcus as being less like a class and more like multiple sets of conversations.[25] Willey said he believed that both he and Tania grew from the experience of teaching together and that she became a broader anthropologist during this period. He also said he admired how Tania continued to develop and change intellectually throughout her career.[26] In Tania's posthumously published *Maya History*, he notes, "[She] was kind enough to collaborate with me in a seminar on Maya art and the interpretations of Maya iconography. I look back on it as an outstanding learning experience for our students and, especially, for me."[27] In a book by Willey and Sabloff, Tania's contribution to the field is explained further: "Traditional archaeology was reinforced by precise and sophisticated stylistic studies, as in Peru and Mesoamerica, by John H. Rowe, Tatiana Proskouriakoff, and George Kubler. All of these scholars brought in ideas from the field of art history, beginning, thereby, some consolidation of the interests and outlooks of American anthropological archaeologists with those of the fine arts school."[28]

In the larger classroom setting where she occasionally had to teach, she was ill at ease. Wren recalled a lecture course given by Tania in 1970 titled "Cosmic Themes in Pre-Columbian Art." It was initially scheduled for a room in the Fogg Museum that would hold thirty students, but on the first day close to one hundred students showed up. Tania entered the room, quietly took out her ashtray, and lit a cigarette. Taking a long drag, she slowly began to speak.[29] Appearances such as this in front of large audiences continued to be difficult for the rest of her life, but to improve her skills as a public speaker, she forced herself to accept more speaking engagements.

In the 1970s Tania became concerned about her increasing "absent-mindedness." She complained of misplacing things that were important to her, for example: "I've lost the jade pamphlet Tozzer had given me and don't remember anything about it."[30] This was particularly alarming to a woman who had been capable of remembering a tremendous number of details, whose mind was described by Sabloff as "encyclopedic."[31]

As the years went on, she felt that time "goes by like the wind."[32] She began to lose close friends, some from among her circle of Cambridge women. One of these was Suzanna Miles, who died of cancer of the tongue. Returning from Guatemala where she had been living and working, Miles rapidly declined as the illness progressed. Tania visited with her frequently, but after one visit, she reflected, "[T]he horror of it leaves me shattered."[33] Writing her friend's obituary, which was published in *American Anthropologist*, Tania observed, "Her untimely death after a year of agonizing illness cut short the career of a scholar of much greater potential stature than her actual accomplishments reveal. . . . Her friends will recall with pleasure and regret their encounters with her agile, observant, and versatile mind."[34] Miles was forty-four years old.

In spite of personal losses, Tania remained active on many levels. She was regularly asked by the editors of various journals to contribute reviews of books and papers on Middle American art and archaeology. Tania's reviews were succinct and clear in their assessments and kept her abreast of new material as it was being published.

In a decision that would affect the future of Maya studies, Tania accepted a request to serve on a committee at the Center for Inter-American Relations in New York. In part as a response to the increased amount of looting of archaeological sites throughout Mesoamerica, the committee met to plan a project to record systematically and publish photographs and drawings of the entire body of Maya hieroglyphic inscriptions. The English explorer Ian Graham, whom Tania had first met in Sayaxché, had conceived of the project and was named its director. Work began immediately on the massive undertaking.[35] Tania provided space in her office at the Peabody, which provided ready access to the important collection of Carnegie Institution photographs of Maya sculpture. Two drafting tables were set up facing the large windows at ground level, and this became Graham's headquarters during the rainy seasons when work in the field became impossible. Since its inception, the project has involved the efforts of Eric von Euw, Peter Mathews, and David Stuart, who have worked together with Graham to produce numerous volumes of the *Corpus of Maya Hieroglyphic Inscriptions*. According to George Stuart of the Center for Maya Research, these publications have become "indispensable as the primary research tool for all present and future students of ancient Maya writing."[36] When we met in his bright, spacious fourth-floor Peabody office, the current project headquarters, Graham said that he will always be grateful for Tania's support of his efforts.[37]

Tania shared with Graham and others in the field a deep concern over the looting of archaeological sites in the Maya region. While at a conference in Los Angeles, she learned that some of the participants were collectors whose pieces included looted antiquities. Outraged, she flew home and withdrew her paper from the subsequent publication.[38] She also was angered by collectors sending her pieces to authenticate. One of these was William Spratling. Trained as an architect, Spratling was known for his beautifully crafted silver jewelry, his bohemian lifestyle, and his large collection of Mexican antiquities on display at his home in Taxco, Mexico. Handsome and charming, he had met Tania during one of her visits to Mexico City.[39] After this the two maintained a friendly correspondence. However, when he later sent her pieces to authenticate, she wrote that she was too "busy" to do this for him. He had crossed a fine line. In his next letter to her, he wrote, "I must tell you that my only regret is that we did not meet many years ago—perhaps by now you would have known me better and to the point where the slander you have been told would not disturb you."[40]

Such encounters resulted in a degree of notoriety with which Tania was ill at ease. Her niece, Norma Ragsdale, recalled that while visiting

Photograph of Tania that appeared on the front page of the *New York Times*, March 28, 1973. Photo by Joyce Dopkeen/NYT Pictures.

with Tania in Cambridge, her telephone was constantly ringing. She said that people frequently requested to interview Tania for films and articles and that she often referred them to the more gregarious Graham.[41] She did, however, agree to an interview with the *New York Times*. The article, which appeared on the front page on March 28, 1973, was titled "Elusive Maya Glyphs Yielding to Modern Technique." It notes her contributions to understanding Maya glyphs and includes her photograph, in which she is leaning jauntily on one of the Maya stelae at the Peabody Museum.

There were some benefits to her increased visibility and reputation. Having attended numerous Mesoamerican conferences over the years at Dumbarton Oaks in Washington, D.C., Tania was asked to serve on the Advisory Committee for Pre-Columbian Art. She accepted the honor and served for two years, the limit in Harvard's mandatory committee retirement policy.[42] Stuart recalled that during one of these conferences, he ferried numerous Mayanists, including Tania and Ignacio Bernal, in his Suburban through hectic Washington traffic from their hotel to the center in Georgetown. He said he was suddenly overwhelmed with the thought, "If a tree falls on us, Maya studies will be in big trouble."[43] A tree did not fall, and the conferences continued to foster new approaches to understanding Mesoamerican cultures.

It was at a Dumbarton Oaks conference in 1971 that Tania presented a paper on her findings concerning the glyphs for bloodletting ceremonies at Yaxchilán. She also heard a paper delivered by Yale University's Floyd Lounsbury, who had been working with Knorosov's phonetic approach to Maya glyphs. Although she did not directly embrace this approach for her own research, she encouraged him to keep at it, much as she had David Kelley.[44]

It was also at Dumbarton Oaks that Tania came into contact with a woman who, like herself, had entered Maya studies through art. This was the energetic, controversial Linda Schele, a woman of vastly different background and personal style from Tania, who would leave her distinct mark on the field before her untimely death in 1999. As described by Elizabeth Benson, then director of the Center for Pre-Columbian Studies at Dumbarton Oaks, the two women sat across from each other at a conference on Mesoamerican writing systems. Tania was reserved but direct and to the point. Schele was flamboyant and outspoken.[45] Tania always dressed carefully for such occasions and was, in the words of her friends, "quite the lady."[46] With her aristocratic bearing, she could seem aloof. Schele, with her southern drawl and blue-jeans coveralls, enjoyed playing up her simple upbringing. It was not a comfortable mix, but the differences ran deeper than style and background.

Tania entered the Maya field quietly, gradually working her way up from drafter-surveyor to one of its leading authorities. Schele burst onto the scene with enthusiasm, passion, and an eagerness to push forward with Maya glyphs. Tania was rigorous in her research and cautious about presenting her results. Offering none of the generous support she had shown other young women entering the field, Tania never got over her distrust of Schele. She remained uncharacteristically and bitterly critical of her and her work.

In 1977 Schele wrote to Tania, "I have been afraid to send material to you partly because I have not wanted to bother you with trivial material and partly because I am afraid of you and your vocal criticism of my work and ethics. My respect for your work and contributions to Maya studies is absolute."[47] After Tania's death, Harvard University, with a gift from Landon T. Clay, established the Tatiana Proskouriakoff Award in 1986 to recognize scholars making contributions "in the field of New World Indian studies, including art, architecture[,] . . . glyphs, language." The first recipient was Linda Schele; others since have included David H. Kelley, Floyd Lounsbury, George Stuart, and Michael Coe.[48]

In the last years of her life, a number of honors were bestowed on Tania. At a ceremony held on the campus at University Park on June 26, 1971, she was presented with the Woman of the Year Award by her alma mater, Pennsylvania State University. On this occasion, Tania had the opportunity to see the tremendous growth and change in the campus since her graduation forty-one years earlier.[49]

In New Orleans on April 14, 1977, Tania received another honor. The ceremony at Tulane University celebrated a significant period for Maya studies, marking fifty-two years since the establishment of the Middle

American Research Institute (MARI). Tania's colleague Robert Wauchope was named emeritus professor in recognition for his work as director of MARI, and Tania was awarded an honorary Doctor of Laws degree, fulfilling a goal she had discussed with Tozzer many years before.[50]

In October 1978, concerned by Tania's weakening health and low morale, Clemency Coggins conceived of a way to give her an emotional boost. She organized a grand tour through Mexico and Guatemala for Tania to see old friends and colleagues. In spite of some difficulties caused by Tania's impaired hearing and eyesight and her occasional forgetfulness, they contacted many people who had been important in her life. In Mexico City they saw, among others, Heinrich Berlin, Alberto Ruz, Isabel Kelley, and Carmen Cook. They heard Ruz give a talk on the history of Maya hieroglyphic decipherment, in which he placed great emphasis on Tania's contributions. Embarrassed, she was asked to take a bow, and according to Coggins, "Afterward, she was lionized by admirers and the press." The visit to Guatemala City also included many old friends, though their time there was marred by political demonstrations. The culmination of this grand tour was a visit to Mérida, where Tania gave a speech in Spanish before a full auditorium at the Universidad de Yucatán.[51]

In the years following this trip, Tania faced more fears about her failing health. She noted, "I can no longer write, and my lines wobble. I keep writhing above them.... Sometimes I think there's something very wrong with my brain."[52] Her eyesight began to deteriorate with retinal degeneration, and walking became increasingly difficult as a result of atherosclerosis brought on by her many years of heavy cigarette smoking.

Her short-term memory also began to be affected, but her long-term memory remained mostly intact, allowing her to continue to work sporadically on a history of the Maya she had begun almost twenty years earlier. Although she felt driven to complete this manuscript, it was not up to the meticulous standards she had set in her previous work. In a review of the posthumously published *Maya History*, Coggins notes with thanks the "dedication and considerable efforts" of all involved in the difficult task of organizing and preparing the material, particularly its final editor, Rosemary Joyce. However, she continues that the lack of area maps and lists of illustrations makes the book difficult for scholars to use. Her most strident criticism comes from the fact that most glyphs under consideration are presented individually and isolated from the context of their inscriptions. In spite of these flaws, Coggins states that Tania's "analytical method is unfailingly instructive, and her observations are dense with suggestive insights. Even where recent readings of inscriptions differ from her interpretations . . . her ideas can seldom be dismissed, and in some cases may prove right in the end."[53]

The last years of Tania's life were a desperate struggle against the ravages of Alzheimer's disease. She continued to receive honors, however. She was elected to membership in the American Philosophical Society "in recognition of signal contributions to important fields of human endeavor." Members of the Philosophical Society are "expected to possess and cherish a humane and philosophical spirit,"[54] making this an especially poignant honor for Tania. With her mental capacities failing, she worked for months to prepare the paper that new members are asked to deliver before the society. In one of the many diary entries that dealt with this, she wrote, "I wasted an entire day rewriting the introduction for my Philosophical Society talk. There are so many ways of saying the same thing!"[55] After finally completing it, she flew to Philadelphia. Her friend Eleanor Easby described Tania presenting "Incidents of Ancient Maya History" on April 21, 1983: "[She wore] a plain black suit—made very special indeed by a collar of heavy handmade lace and an antique brooch. . . . On that visit Chris Jones gave her one of the first copies of his and Linton Satterthwaite's *Monuments and Inscriptions of Tikal*, which he'd dedicated to her and to the memory of Sylvanus Morley and Eric Thompson."[56] It was a grand homecoming for Tania that would have inspired many memories of the happy years she had spent there. She would rise to such an occasion one more time in her life.

In fall 1984, after she had been moved to the Emerson Convalescent Home in nearby Watertown, Massachusetts, Tania was picked up and driven to the Peabody Museum. In an intimate ceremony, the Honorable Federico Fahsen, Guatemalan ambassador to the United States, conferred on Tania the Order of the Quetzal for her contributions to the

Guatemalan ambassador, Federico Fahsen, presenting Tania with the Order of the Quetzal, Guatemala's highest honor, at the Peabody Museum, 1984. Courtesy of President & Fellows of Harvard College, Peabody Museum, Harvard University (N 34820).

study of pre-Columbian art, architecture, and hieroglyphs. It is Guatemala's highest honor. Among those present were her good friends Gordon Willey, Ledyard Smith, Ian Graham, Peter Mathews, Richard Townsend, and Clemency Coggins.[57]

It was a most fitting honor, but as Tania's illness progressed, she had difficulty relishing even this. In the nursing home where Coggins and Graham had helped to place her, Tania began to experience delusions that Guatemalan guerrilla fighters had kidnapped her.[58] Her one overwhelming desire was to return home to her apartment, but this was impossible. Still a persistent chain-smoker, she frequently forgot she had lit a cigarette. She had become a danger to herself and to others in the building. Although friends continued to stop by to see her, she wrote, "The last thoughts of my life are gloomy. How can one live without sight, without books, without a typewriter? And even worse without friends? The honors being awarded me for past accomplishments should cheer me, but they only emphasize that all are in the past and what confronts me now is darkness; loneliness and regret. It was doubtless my fault, though not my intention that I am . . ."[59] This last sentence remained unfinished. On August 30, 1985, at the age of seventy-six, Tania died.[60] Obituaries appeared in the *Boston Globe* and the *New York Times*. Not the solitary figure she perceived herself, many friends and colleagues mourned her passing. Among these was one who would see to it that her ashes were returned to the jungle she so loved.

CHAPTER TWELVE

The Ceremony of the Ashes (1998)

In May 1997 I sat across the table from Ian Graham, surrounded by photographs and drawings of monuments and hieroglyphic inscriptions, in his office at the Peabody Museum. It was the first time I had seen him in more than twenty years and my first chance to speak with him face-to-face since beginning to write about Tania. From the list of questions I had for him, I asked where Tania had been buried. He said with a twinkle in his eye, "Why, she is right here." Knowing I was in for a tale, I began taking notes. The story he related to me that day is this.

After her death, in the tradition of her family, Tania's remains were cremated. A person from the mortuary called to say that her ashes were ready to be picked up. It was a gray day, with "a fine Scotch mist," the sort of day Graham enjoys taking long, brisk walks. When he got to the establishment, he entered and was given a lily-patterned paper bag with handles. In it was a metal canister containing Tania's ashes. With the bag in hand, Graham headed toward the subway entrance several blocks away. It began to rain harder; and by the time he reached the subway, he was quite wet. He took the train to Park Street Station, where he had to change lines. As he stepped off the train, the damp bag ripped. The container fell to the floor, and his foot hit it. He watched as it skittered across the platform and came to rest close to its edge, just as a train came in. He hastily picked it up, wrapped the ripped bag around the container, and entered the train, hoping that no one had identified it. Once back at his office, he carefully placed it in one of his cabinet drawers for safe-keeping.

Graham considered scattering Tania's ashes from a boat at Lake Win-nepesaukee, New Hampshire. It had been such a special place to Tania, a peaceful retreat from the hectic pace of city life. It would be a fitting place, and she would have approved. However, the longer he thought about it, the more the image of another place came to his mind, and it was for this that he waited. The wait would last more than a decade, for political tensions along the Usumacinta River made it unsafe for travel to Piedras Negras, the place most fitting for Tania's ashes. Graham con-cluded his story by saying that the area was again accessible and that within a year either he or David Stuart would make the trip.[1]

In April 1998 Stuart fulfilled this promise. In an interview, he explained that he needed to go to Piedras Negras to take photographs of the inscriptions and to make a final check on-site for a volume he was preparing for the *Corpus of Maya Hieroglyphic Inscriptions*. He flew to Mérida, carrying with him the container with Tania's ashes. From there he drove to Tenosique to join with others from the project that was currently under way at Piedras Negras. Codirected by Stephen Houston and Héctor Escobedo, this project was staffed by Americans from the University of Pennsylvania, Brigham Young University, Yale Univer-sity, and Tania's alma mater, Pennsylvania State University. They worked with Guatemalans from the Universidad del Valle. Stuart and others from the project made the six-hour hike from the Mexican border to the site. They followed the valley that runs parallel to the Usumacinta River, along the same route cleared during Satterthwaite's expeditions more than fifty years earlier.[2]

With permission from Guatemala's Institute of Archaeology and His-tory, Stuart conferred with Houston and Escobedo to determine the spot most appropriate for burying Tania's ashes. They agreed on a location at the summit of the Acropolis, in structure J-23. It is seen as the highest structure in Tania's famous reconstruction drawing of Piedras Negras, printed in countless publications over the years.

Once the appropriate spot for the ashes was chosen, several members of the project cleared debris from the surface of the original plaster floor. They cut a rectangular area through the floor and excavated a small hole. The next afternoon the entire team gathered in the camp and in a silent procession slowly made the twenty-five-minute walk through the jungle. Other than the presence of a rusted tractor left behind years before, little had changed since Tania described the setting in her *Album*: "The principal approach is by a single, broad stairway, flanked by two pyramidal structures and by long platforms supporting rows of stelae. The stairway leads to a building of many doorways, through which one enters an enclosed quadrangle, surrounded by higher terraces and rectangular buildings. Beyond this, two more courts at still higher levels rise to the crest of the composition, a small palace overlooking the river flowing nearly three hundred feet below."[3] It was to the remains of this "small palace" that the procession wound its way.

With a breeze gently stirring the leaves of the surrounding trees, the group gathered silently. Standing near the excavated hole, now adorned with two simple bouquets of rain forest flowers and greenery, Stuart began to speak quietly. He said that they had brought Tania's ashes to her final resting place. He continued that it was appropriate they should be at the pinnacle of the site to honor someone who "stands at the pinnacle of Maya studies" and who had "revolutionized the field, not only through her work with glyphs, but also through her graceful artistry."[4] A young Guatemalan scholar, Monica Urquizú, next spoke in Spanish of Tania's importance as a role model to women in archaeology. Héctor Escobedo followed, saying that he was proud to have Tania's remains in Guatemala, where she had made such outstanding contributions in her field.

The container was placed in the hole, and each person present quietly placed a stone inside to refill the cavity. After several attempts to light it, copal was burned and smoke was blown into Tania's burial place. Finally, using hats and shin protectors as shovels, earth was scooped up and used to completely fill in around the stones. There was a call of a single bird, as the loose dirt was gently patted down and covered by the piece of stucco floor. Over this were placed the rain forest bouquets.

In this touchingly simple ceremony, held thirteen years after her death, there is a sense of closure, of coming full circle. Tania leaves behind a legacy of intellectual curiosity, and through her steadfast adherence to rigorous scholarship, she showed that even the most widely held assumptions can, and should, be questioned. In her articles and books, she challenges us to look deeper, to expand our knowledge of ancient Maya civilization, and perhaps through them, come to a greater understanding of our own. Most eloquently, Escobedo concluded the ceremony by saying that although Tania did not "leave biological descendants, we who continue her work, her intellectual children, we are her true heirs."[5]

NOTES

ABBREVIATIONS

CCC	Clemency C. Coggins' personal file on Tatiana Proskouriakoff
CIW	Carnegie Institution of Washington
LS	Linton Satterthwaite
PMA	Peabody Museum Archives, Harvard University
PPP	Private Proskouriakoff Family Papers
TP	Tatiana Proskouriakoff
TPMA	Transcription of taped conversation with Tatiana Proskouriakoff, made by Monni Adams in 1982.
UpennMA	University of Pennsylvania Museum Archives, University of Pennsylvania

CHAPTER ONE

1. Tatiana Proskouriakoff (hereafter TP) diary entry, February 13, 1939. All personal diaries of Tatiana Proskouriakoff are housed at the Harvard University Archives, Pusey Library, Harvard University (HUGFP 51.xx).

2. Biographical details of Tania's parents are found in the family's private Proskouriakoff papers (hereafter cited as PPP) and a 1983 taped conversation between TP and her aunt, Mila Chenzoff made by Mike Beetem, Tania's nephew. Beetem made the papers and the tape available to the author.

3. Moynahan 1994, 49–50.

4. Coe 1992, 167; Hughes 1998, 454.

5. T. Proskouriakoff interview (transcription) by Monni Adams, 1982, 997–245 (in 993-25 Box 1.1a), Peabody Museum Archives, Harvard University (hereafter cited as TPMA).

6. Moynahan 1994, 14; Canning 1923, 160.

7. Graham 1990, 7.

8. TPMA.

9. Dukes 1974, 200.

10. From a story related by TP at Thanksgiving dinner with Clemency C. Coggins and her family. Coggins graciously made her personal file on Tania available to me (hereafter cited as CCC).

11. Riasanovsky 1977, 455.

12. Graham 1990, 7.

13. Canning 1923, 127.

14. This story of the family's attempt to leave Russia is compiled from Graham 1990, 7; and TPMA.

15. "World War I," Microsoft ® Encarta ® 97 Encyclopedia. © 1993–96 Microsoft Corporation.

16. PPP.

17. TPMA.

CHAPTER TWO

1. PPP. This cruise booklet compiled by the Norwegian America Line is among the personal items in a leather scrapbook put together by Alla Proskouriakoff.

2. CCC.

3. TPMA.

4. Tania's cigarette smoking was noted by many of her friends and colleagues, but this anecdote came from Sean Eirik Simpson in a telephone interview, March 28, 1999, and CCC.

5. PPP.

6. Interview with Andrew Chenzoff, October 29, 1998.

7. Tania told this story over lunch to her friend Barbara Page, who wrote it down for the *Proskouriakoff Scrapbook* compiled by Ian Graham, n.d. Accession currently pending. It is housed at the Peabody Museum Archives, Harvard University (hereafter cited as PMA).

8. Joyce Marcus, personal correspondence with author, August 31, 1997.

9. TPMA.

10. Chandler and Salsbury 1971, 372; Hatch 1956, 224.

11. "1917 Eddystone Blast Still a Mystery," *Philadelphia Inquirer*, April 9, 1967.

12. PPP: "Index. Eddystone Ammunition Corp. Morgan Order. A. P. Proskouriakoff, Inspector."

13. TPMA.

14. PPP.

15. Telephone interview with Frank Harrison, August 15, 1997.

16. Mead 1972, 72.

17. Membership, 1904–56, Lansdowne Monthly meeting of the Religious Society of Friends, Friends Historical Library of Swarthmore College.

18. Josephine McCall's entry, *Proskouriakoff Scrapbook*, n.d. Accession currently pending, PMA; interview with Andrew Chenzoff, October 29, 1998.

19. Telephone interview with Boris Nekrassoff, July 20, 1997, and with Tania's niece, Norma Jean Ragsdale, March 7, 1998.

20. TP diary entry, February 10, 1941.

21. Josephine McCall's entry, *Proskouriakoff Scrapbook*, n.d. Accession currently pending, PMA

22. Obituary, *Friends Intelligencer*, April 25, 1953.

23. Interview with Andrew Chenzoff, October 29, 1998, and taped conversation between TP and Mila Chenzoff, PPP.

24. *Garnet and Gray*, 1926, Lansdowne High School's yearbook. In a telephone interview on August 15, 1997, Matthew Schultz, of the Lansdowne Historical Society, explained McClatchy was a local commercial developer in the 1920s. Schultz also kindly provided leads on old residents of Lansdowne and located a copy of the yearbook.

CHAPTER THREE

1. *Garnet and Gray*, 1926.

2. Telephone interview with Linnea Wren, July 19, 1997.

3. Bezilla 1985, 124.

4. TPMA.

5. Shenk 1932, 405.

6. TPMA.

7. Bezilla 1985, 152.

8. Ibid., 123.

9. From various telephone interviews with Joyce Marcus and conversations with Clemency Coggins between 1997 and 2000.

10. From the Penn State yearbook, *LaVie*, 1926–30.

11. TPMA.

12. TP diary entry, February 17, 1946.

13. TP diary entry, October 9, 1949.

14. Polly Margolf's entry, *Proskouriakoff Scrapbook*, n.d. Accession currently pending, PMA.

15. TPMA.

16. Evans 1998, 218.

17. College page of *Proskouriakoff Scrapbook*, n.d. Accession currently pending, PMA.

18. TP diary entry, May 20, 1941.

19. TP diary entry, June 18, 1940.

20. TP diary entry, July 16, 1940.

21. Concerts on this magnificent organ are still given daily at Lord & Taylor's.

22. TP diary entry, July 27, 1949.

23. This story and all information on Sinkler's Studio came from numerous telephone interviews. These were with Catherine Hunt, who purchased the business from Mrs. Sinkler; Holly Reed, who worked with Mila at the studio; and Mila's son, Andrew Chenzoff.

24. TPMA.

25. *The Ledger*, December 9, 1930. Alex Pezzatti, archivist of the University of Pennsylvania Museum Archives, kindly brought this article to my attention.

CHAPTER FOUR

1. This anecdote comes from a letter to the author by Linnea Wren dated July 31, 1997. Other stories of Tania's humor come from Sean Eirik Simpson, Ian Graham, Joyce Marcus, and Monni Adams.

2. Stuart in Danien and Sharer 1992, 14–17; Brunhouse 1973, 86–88.

3. Black 1990, 257–60.

4. Madeira 1964, 15–44.

5. Mercer 1975, 58–64, 85–97.

6. Berg 1998, 208–10.

7. "Archaeologist to Discuss Expeditions," *Public Ledger,* December 14, 1930.

8. This quote about Linton Satterthwaite (hereafter cited as LS) is from an introductory speech given on April 10, 1999, by George Stuart at the 17th Annual Maya Weekend, University Museum of the University of Pennsylvania.

9. Bourne 1919, 315.

10. William Haviland, Christopher Jones, Linton Satterthwaite Thorn (nephew of LS), and Alice Laquer (niece of LS) all contributed the biographical information on Satterthwaite through correspondence and telephone interviews.

11. Shook 1998, 224.

12. This version of how Tania and Satterthwaite met is from TPMA and numerous conversations with Joyce Marcus, Chris Jones, and Ed Shook.

13. Linton Satterthwaite kept careful copies of all his correspondence, now at the University of Pennsylvania Museum Archives (hereafter cited as UPennMA). This letter to Tania is dated February 19, 1936.

14. O'Neill 1998.

15. TPMA.

16. Descriptions of this Piedras Negras expedition are from the diary by Margaret C. Satterthwaite (1931), UPennMA, Piedras Negras Expedition, Box 10.

17. Biographical sketch by TP, Box 1.1, Proskouriakoff Papers 993-25, PMA.

18. Interview with David Stuart, April 9, 1999.

19. Telephone interview with Peter Mathews, September 30, 1998.

20. TPMA.

21. The cocktail hour was described in interviews with Joyce Marcus and Ian Graham; of Tania's dress and the story about ironing Linton's shirts came from Joyce Marcus in a personal communication.

22. Shook 1998, 51–58.

23. Compiled from interviews with Christopher Jones, Sean Eirik Simpson, and William Haviland.

24. Letter from LS to TP, June 8, 1943, UPennMA.

25. The information on women in the field is from an interview with Jeremy Sabloff, director of the University Museum, October 31, 1997. Some of the women who have cited Tania's influence on their careers are Joyce Marcus of the University of Michigan, Clemency Coggins of Boston University, Linnea Wren of Gustavus Adolphus College, Jessica Child of Yale University, and Monica Urquizú of the Universidad del Valle.

26. Satterthwaite 1943, 6.

27. TP letter to LS, September 10, [1937], UpennMA.

28. Satterthwaite 1943, 9, and verified by Carol Spawn, archivist, Academy of Natural Science, Philadelphia.

29. Interview with David Stuart, May 15, 1998.

CHAPTER FIVE

1. TPMA.

2. Interview with Jerry Sabloff, October 31, 1997.

3. Letter from Morley to L. N. Cotlow, September 6, 1939, from the Collection of Khristaan D. Villela, Santa Fe, New Mex.

4. Carnegie 1920, 260; Brunhouse 1971, 63–65.

5. This story about Morley's "discovery" of Tania and his subsequent funding of her first expedition is from TPMA and Brunhouse 1975, 275.

6. TPMA.

7. Willey 1988, 294–313.

8. TPMA.

9. TP diary entry, February 15, 1939.

10. TP diary entry, February 18, 1939.

11. TP diary entry, February 20, 1939.

12. Letter from TP to J. Alden Mason, March 10, 1939, American Philosophical Society Library, Philadelphia.

13. TP diary entry, February 21, 1939.

14. TP diary entry, February 22, 1939.

15. TP diary entry, February 23, 1939.

16. TPMA.

17. TP diary entry, February 23, 1939.

18. Telephone interviews and correspondence with John Longyear, 1998–2000.

19. TPMA.

20. TPMA.

21. TP diary entry, January 21, 1941.

22. TPMA.

23. Olaf Husby, a Norwegian linguist who is working on a biography of Strömsvik, kindly provided all Strömsvik's early biographical information.

24. Information on Strömsvik's engineering feats is from the author's correspondence and telephone interviews with John Longyear and from Shook 1998, 215–23.

25. TP diary entry, February 24, 1939.

26. Gustav Strömsvik field notebook 1939, Copán. Carnegie Institution of Washington (CIW) Records, 58–34, Box III–III#3, PMA.

27. TP diary entry, February 28, 1939.

28. Strömsvik, field notebook, 1939, Copán, PMA.

29. John Longyear made available a copy of his 8mm film shot in Copán on numerous trips, including 1939. It is currently with Longyear's personal papers and records.

30. TP diary entry, February 26, 1939.

31. TP diary entry, March 1, 1939.

32. TP diary entry, March 3, 1939.

33. TP diary entry, March 6, 1939.

34. Interviews and correspondence with John Longyear, 1998–2000.

35. TP diary entry, March 7, 1939.

36. TP diary entry, March 18, 1939.

37. Shook 1998, 221.

38. TP diary entry, March 26, 1939.

39. Letter from TP to LS, undated, 1939, UPennMA.

40. TP diary entry, March 23, 1939.

41. TP diary entry, April 9, 1939.

42. TP diary entry, April 19, 1939.

43. Shook 1998, 231–34; and correspondence with John Longyear.

44. TP diary entry, April 19, 1939.

45. Morris 1974, 448–50; Bishop and Lange 1991, x–xi, 1–33; Parezo 1993, 208–10.

46. Letter from TP to Alden Mason, March 10, 1939, American Philosophical Society Library.

47. Letter from TP to LS, undated, UPennMA. It is handwritten on Carnegie Institution, Copán Project, stationary.

48. TP diary entry, April 19, 1939.

49. TP diary entry, April 27, 1939.

50. TP diary entry, April 30, 1939.

51. Descriptions of Cobán and the surrounding area come from Brigham [1887] 1965, 91–102; and Cipriani 1998, 130–34.

52. TP diary entry, May 2, 1939.

53. Hay et al. [1940] 1977, 250; Satterthwaite 1943, 5.

54. TP diary entry, May 3, 1939.

55. TP diary entry, May 8, 1939

56. TP diary entry, May 8, 1939

57. TP diary entry, May 8, 1939.

CHAPTER SIX

1. Letter from TP to Alden Mason, July 5, 1939, American Philosophical Library.

2. TP diary entry, September 6, 1939.

3. TP diary entries, September 9–14 and November 17, 1939.

4. TP diary entry, September 15, 1939.

5. TP diary entry, September 16, 1939.

6. TP diary entry, September 30, 1939.

7. TP diary entry, September 17, 1939.

8. TP Diary entry, September 21, 1939.

9. TP diary entry, September 25, 1939.

10. TP diary entry, September 26, 1939.

11. Telephone interviews and correspondence, Mike Beetem and Norma Jean Ragsdale.

12. TP diary entry, October 12, 1939,

13. TP diary entry, October 19, 1939.

14. Ed Shook, telephone interview, January 27, 1997.

15. TP diary entry, October 29, 1939.

16. TP diary entry, November 16, 1939.

17. For his descriptions of World War II and its impact on Guatemala, see Shook 1998, 79-94. The effects on Mexico can be found in Herring 1972, 367–69.

18. There is an excellent description of the Carnegie headquarters at Chichén in O'Neill 1998, 14–15; and Brunhouse 1971, 208–19.

19. Telephone interview, Fernando Barbachano, January 26, 2000. There is no diary of Tania's 1940 field season, but details can be pieced together from her later diaries and her field notebook (CIW Records, 58-34, Proskouriakoff 1940, Chichen-Uxmal [III-2 #6], PMA).

20. There is an informative Web site on Maya architecture by Barbara McKenzie with current photos. A description of the ruins of Uxmal is in Harris and Ritz 1993, 183–87; and an account of the history of the study of Maya architecture is in Hay et al. [1940] 1977, 180–97.

21. Some of the descriptions of conditions for working in Yucatán are from my personal journals 1972–76, as well as from Stuart and Stuart 1977, 90.

22. Interview with Ian Graham, April 29, 1997.

23. TP letter to Bonnie Rorrer, March 7, 1980, used with permission from Ms. Rorrer.

24. TP diary entry, May 26, 1941.

25. TP diary entries, June 4 and 8, 1940.

26. The lunch club was a continuing pleasure for Tania though the participants varied over the years. This description is from TP diary entry, June 13, 1940.

27. TP diary entries, June 11 and 19, 1940. Pollock describes Landa as an exceptional source "of so much of our knowledge of Maya culture" in Hay [1940] 1977, 180.

28. TP diary entry, June 17, 1940.

29. TP diary entry, June 26, 1940.

30. TP diary entries, June 25 and 28, 1940.

31. TP diary entries, July 3, 1940.

32. Letter from TP to LS, July 21, 1940, UPennMA, LS Records.

33. TP diary entries, July 6–11, 1940.

34. Fadiman 1939, 109.

35. Graham 1990, 8-9; Shook 1998, 226.

36. Tania found dinners with the Kochs very stimulating and discovered she was formulating definite political views such as those expressed in TP diary entry, July 1, 1940.

37. The first time Tania mentions the Quakers in her diaries is August 4, 1940. They would become increasingly important to Tania during the war.

38. TP diary entry, July 1, 1940.

39. The fountain Tania designed for Copán was built and still stands in the square at Copán Village, although it no longer functions. In correspondence of September 24, 1999, with Barbara Fash, I learned that in the early 1990s there was an attempt to get it to work again. With Alfonso Morales, they installed a small pump and some white lights. Fash writes, "It was fine for a day, until the mayor . . . installed colored lights and a larger pump. It ran like a light show for a few days with water pouring out instead of the slow trickle we had installed. Then it burned out the pump . . . so it is back to its quiet state."

40. TP diary entry, August 25, 1940.

41. TP diary entry, January 11, 1941.

42. TP diary entry, February 10, 1941.

43. TP diary entry, February 10, 1941.

44. TP diary entry, March 25, 1941. Throughout that winter, Tania wrote increasingly about the Quaker meetings in Cambridge.

45. TP diary entry, undated [between May 26 and July 19, 1941].

46. TP diary entry, July 20, 1941.

47. TP diary entry, March 25, 1941.

48. TP diary entry, May 20, 1941.

49. TP diary entry, May 26, 1941.

50. TP diary entry, July 31, 1941.

51. TP diary entries, November 9 and October 19, 1941.

52. TP diary entry, December 7, 1941.

53. TP diary entry, January 6, 1941.

54. TP diary entry, February 26, 1941.

55. TP diary entry, June 17, 1942.

56. TPMA.

57. TP diary entry, April 10, 1943.

58. TP diary entry, June 16, 1942, contains information about several of the Carnegie archaeologists and their wartime activities.

59. Shook 1998, 81–94.

60. Willey 1988, 347.

61. Shook 1998, 83.

62. TP diary entry, June 16, 1942.

63. TP diary entry, October 10, 1942, covers information on Ruppert and Boggs. Information on Andrews's enlistment is from a telephone conversation with Joann Andrews, December 2, 1999; the information on John Longyear is from his correspondence with the author, December 10, 1999.

64. Correspondence with Olaf Husby, 1997–99.

65. TP diary entry, April 10, 1943.

66. This little-known fact about Tania taking a ship-drafting class in Boston is found in TP diary entry, October 5, 1942.

67. TP diary entry, October 27, 1942. Tania's entry in her diary about her father's death is extensive. I have quoted only one portion.

68. TP diary entries, July 29, 1944, and August 6, 1944. In these passages it is clear that it was pleasing to Tania to play the piano again. In 1973, when I was working as a volunteer on Tania's jade catalog, she asked me how I liked living in Cambridge. I told her I missed having a piano to practice on. Without indicating that she knew how to play or that she had experienced a similar situation earlier in her life, she wrote a letter on my behalf to the Harvard music department suggesting that I be given access to the practice rooms. It was a kind gesture and one I appreciated greatly.

69. TP diary entry, February 4, 1943. This is just one of many references to concerts Tania attended, often performed by the Boston Symphony.

70. TP diary entry, May 6, 1942.

71. TP diary entry November 22, 1943, deals with Anna Shepard.

72. TP diary entry October 20, 1943.

73. *CIW Year Book No. 42*, July 1, 1942–June 30, 1943, 185–86.

74. Letter from TP to J. Alden Mason, August 9, 1943, American Philosophical Society Library.

75. TP diary entry, August 5, 1944.

76. *CIW Yearbook No. 43*, July 1, 1943–June 30, 1944, 169.

77. This quote from Ed Shook is taken from a telephone interview with Shook on September 28, 1997.

CHAPTER SEVEN

1. TPMA.

2. Shook article in *Ancient Mesoamerica* 1, no. 2 (1990): 249.

3. *CIW Year Book No. 44*, 166.

4. TPMA.

5. TP diary entry, "Sunday Late October," 1944.

6. TP diary entry, November 2, 1944.

7. Clemency Coggins, Joyce Marcus, and Sean Eirik Simpson all mentioned in interviews Tania's passion for mystery books. There were periods in her life when she thought about writing mysteries.

8. TP diary entry, "Sunday Late October," 1944.

9. Weinberg 1994, 505–6; Buckley 1984, 64–65; Shook 1998, 254–55. "Free elections": Burns 1994, 265–66.

10. Tania's efforts to get Alla to move to Cambridge were hampered by Alla's desire to practice medicine, something she could do in Pennsylvania but was denied in Massachusetts. There are several diary entries dealing with Tania's frustration over this matter; this quote comes from TP diary entry, November 11, 1943.

11. TP diary entry, January 1, 1945.

12. Based on his trip, Kirk Bryan produced a report on soil and climate in Guatemala that was included in the *CIW Yearbook No. 44*, 168–70.

13. Letter from TP to Linton Satterthwaite, January 12, 1945, UpennMA, LS folder.

14. TP diary entry, January 8, 1945.

15. TP diary entry, April 7, 1944. In a telephone interview in August 1997, Norma Ragsdale recalled that both Tania and Kay had their voting privileges revoked during the war. This may be the incident she heard about in family stories.

16. Description of the approach to Guatemala City by air is recalled from my own experience. Information on the capital is from Harris 1993, 298.

17. TP letter to Kay Beetem, January 31, 1945, PPP.

18. TP field notebook, January 29, 1945, CIW Records 58-34, Proskouriakoff, T., 1945, III-2#6, PMA.

19. Stuart and Stuart 1977, 26–27; Shook 1998, 98, 211–12; Harris and Ritz 1993, 303–4; Coe 1999, 50–51, 66–72.

20. TP field notebook, February 1, 1945, CIW Records 58-34, Proskouriakoff, T., 1945, III-2#6, PMA.

21. Biographical information on A. Ledyard Smith is from interviews with his son, Ledyard, Jr.; Willey 1988, 365–68; Shook 1998, 24–25, 35–40.

22. Sharer 1994, 180–81; Shook 1998, 33–40; Black 1990, 258–59.

23. Interview with Ledyard Smith Jr., August 8, 1999.

24. *CIW Year Book No. 44*, 166.

25. *CIW Year Book No. 44*, 165.

26. TP field notebook, February 7, 1945, CIW Records 58-34, Proskouriakoff, T., 1945, III-2#6, PMA; Sharer 1994, 26; Harris and Ritz 1993, 312–13.

27. Willey 1988, 368; Shook 1998, 209; interview with Ledyard Smith Jr., October 30, 2000.

28. Lothrop 1948, 77. This quaint book by Eleanor Lothrop gives her perspective of life as an archaeologist's wife and contains illustrations by Miguel Covarrubias.

29. A. V. Kidder Diary entries, February 1, 4, 7, 1945, Harvard University Archives, Pusey Library.

30. Letter from Ginny and Ed Shook to TP, April 9, 1945, from the personal papers of Edwin M. Shook, used with his permission.

31. TP field notebook, February 14–18, 1945, CIW Records 58-34, Proskouriakoff, T., 1945, III-2#6, PMA.

32. Foster 1997, 81–84; Whipperman 1995, 450–52.

33. TP field notebook, February 14–18, 1945, CIW Records 58-34, Proskouriakoff, T., 1945, III-2#6, PMA.

34. TP field notebook, February 19, 1945, CIW Records, 58-34 Proskouriakoff, T., 1945, III-2#6, PMA.

35. Smith 1996, 119; Foster 1997, 53; Mallan 1994, 373.

36. Description of travel to El Tajín and time around Mexico City: TP field notebook, February 24–March 2, 1945, CIW Records 58-34, Box III-2 6, PMA; and letter from TP to Ed Shook, February 23, 1945, Shook's personal papers.

37. Telephone conversation with Kornelia Kurbjuhn, March 10, 2000. Also, Henning Siverts correspondence with author, March 13, 2000.

38. Letter from TP to Ed Shook, April 3, 1945, Shook's personal papers.

39. Letter from TP to Ed Shook, April 3, 1945, Shook's personal papers.

40. Williams 1994, 155.

41. "Act of Chapultepec," Microsoft ® Encarta ® 97 Encyclopedia. © 1993–96 Microsoft Corporation.

42. TP diary entry, April 13, 1945.

43. TP diary entry, June 27, 1945.

44. Letter from TP to Ed Shook, July 20, 1945, Shook's personal papers.

45. TP diary entry, January 26, 1946.

46. Anna Shephard letter to TP, April 30, 1946, from the collection of Tania's personal correspondence currently held by Sean Eirik Simpson (hereafter cited as Simpson Collection).

47. According to her diary entry of January 8, 1943, after reading the draft of her manuscript for the *Album*, Kidder released Tania from half of her drafting duties to pursue her own work.

48. TP diary entry, February 17, 1946.

49. Zimmer 1951, 8; TP diary entry, August 22, 1946.

50. TP diary entry, August 30, 1946.

51. Information about Bush's eventual shutting down of the Division of Historical Research is from Shook 1998, 103–5; Givens 1992, 114–15; and Woodbury 1973, 70–72.

52. TP diary entry, July 1, 1945.

53. TPMA.

54. TP diary entry, September 15, 1946.

55. *CIW Year Book No. 46*, 173.

56. Miller 1995, 55–56.

57. TP diary entry, August 27, 1946.

58. TP diary entry, September 21, 1946.

59. *CIW Year Book No. 46*, 177.

60. TP diary entries, January 23, 25, and 27, 1947.

61. Brunhouse 1971, 284; *CIW Year Book No. 46*, 176. Tania's visit with Morley to Uxmal: TP diary entry, January 28, 1947.

62. TP diary entry, February 3, 1947.

63. *CIW Year Book No. 46*, 175.

64. On Tania's travels with Alla: TP diary entries, February 3–13, 1947; for the direct quote about Alla: TP diary entry, January 26, 1947.

65. TP diary entry, February 17, 1947.

66. TP diary entry, February 15, 1947.

67. TP diary entry, March 1–2, 1947.

68. The sites visited are found in *CIW Year Book No. 46*, 184. Tania's drawings were published in Ledyard Smith's *Archaeological Reconnaissance in Central Guatemala*, CIW Pub. 608.

69. TP diary entry, March 8, 1947.

70. TP diary entry, February 22, 1947.

71. TP diary entries, April 7 and 14, 1947.

72. Ledyard Smith's entry, *Proskouriakoff Scrapbook*, n.d. Accession currently pending, PMA.

73. TP diary entry, March 22, 1947.

74. Health matters: TP diary entries, April 24–30, 1947.

75. TP diary entries, April 7 and 14, 1947.

CHAPTER EIGHT

1. Manuscript: TP diary entries November 13, 14, and 16, 1947.

2. Brunhouse 1971, 226–27; Danien and Sharer 1992, 33–35; Coe 1992, 124–26.

3. Shook 1998, 229–30.

4. Letter from J. Eric S. Thompson to Tania, dated Ground Hog Day, 1948, Simpson Collection.

5. *CIW Year Book No. 47*, 210.

6. The suggestion of Tania's early shyness is from telephone interviews with Ed Shook, and the perception of Tania in the early years at the Carnegie offices is from telephone interviews with Richard Woodbury, February 10 and March 27, 2000.

7. *CIW Year Book No. 47*, 210.

8. TP diary entry, November 14, 1947. These evenings are described intermittently in Tania's diaries until June 1948.

9. Proskouriakoff 1950, iii.

10. TP diary entry, November 22, 1947.

11. TP diary entry, November 13, 1947.

12. TP diary entry, November 22, 1947.

13. Interviews with Ledyard Smith Jr., August 7, 1999, and October 30, 2000.

14. TP diary entry, February 12, 1948.

15. Willey 1988, 368; *CIW Year Book No. 48*, 225.

16. TP diary entry, January 29, 1949.

17. TP diary entry, November 22, 1949.

18. TP diary entry, January 20, 1949.

19. TP diary entry, July 27, 1949.

20. *CIW Year Book No. 48*, 218.

21. Chadha 1997, 462–76; TP diary entry, January 30, 1948.

22. Yagoda 1993, 295.

23. TP diary entry, March 21, 1948.

24. Web site of the U.S. Department of Energy Office of Environmental Management Historical Document. Time line, August 1949 and the 1950s.

25. TP diary entry, January 25, 1949.

26. Willey 1988, 266–90.

27. TP diary entries, January 21–22, 1949.

28. TP diary entry, July 30, 1949.

29. TP diary entry, August 6, 1949.

30. Letter from TP to Kay Beetem, August 31, 1949, PPP.

31. *CIW Year Book No. 49*, 193.

32. Letter from LS to TP, October 11, 1951, Simpson Collection.

33. Letter from LS to TP, November 10, 1952, Simpson Collection.

34. Letter from TP to Kay Beetem, January 8, 1950, PPP. In an interview with Jo's son, Marsh MacCall, on August 24, 2000, he described the delight these two old friends took in seeing each other.

35. Letter from TP to Kay Beetem, January 15, 1950, PPP.

36. TP diary entry, February 9, 1950.

37. TP diary entry, February 26, 1950.

38. TP diary entry, March 2, 1950.

39. TP diary entry, March 4, 1950.

40. TP diary entries, March 8–12, 1950.

41. Letter from TP to Kay Beetem, undated, PPP.

42. Tania's colleague, who suggested alternate travel to El Tajín, was Barlow. TP diary entry, March 6, 1950.

43. TP diary entries, March 28 and April 4, 1950.

44. TP diary entry, April 7, 1950.

45. TP diary entry, April 21, 1950.

46. Letter from TP to Kay Beetem, undated, PPP.

47. TP diary entry, September 7, 1950.

48. TP diary entry, December 13, 1950.

49. TP diary entry, September 13, 1950.

50. TP diary entry, December 13, 1950.

51. TP diary entry, October 17, 1950.

52. Quotes on Tozzer: TP diary entries, January 15, 1951, November 27, 1950, December 13, 1950, and April 21, 1950. Also, Willey 1988, 286.

53. Woodbury 1973, 81. Also, telephone interview with Richard Woodbury, July 5, 2000, and correspondence from Woodbury, July 6, 2000.

54. Letter from TP to Kay Beetem, September 30, 1950, PPP.

55. "Group Readies Awards for 300 Years," *Boston Herald*, November 2, 1950.

56. TP letter to Kay Beetem, November 14, 1950, PPP.

57. Letter from LS to TP, January 11, 1951, UpennMA, LS file.

58. Sarah Turner, archivist at the American Institute of Architects Library, provided the information on Igor Polevitzsky. Tania's description of her visit with him is from TP diary entry, March 24, 1951.

59. *CIW Year Book No. 47*, 207.

60. 1951 field season: TP diary entries, January 1951–May 1951. Also, *CIW Year Book No. 50,* 225–26, 236–37.

61. These S-shaped benches, called "confidenciales," intrigued Tania. Harris and Ritz 1993, 163.

62. That Harry Pollock began to rely on Tania becomes evident in many diary entries beginning June 12, 1951.

63. Letter from Alla Proskouriakoff to Kay Beetem, September 1, 1951, PPP. Their trip to Mexico is described in detail in Alla's journal of the trip, PPP.

64. Letter from TP to Ed and Ginny Shook, August 19, 1951, Shook's personal papers.

65. Letter from Alla to Kay Beetem, December 14, 1951, PPP.

66. Letter from TP to Kay Beetem, undated, PPP.

67. Final letter from Alla to Kay Beetem, January 4, 1952, PPP.

68. Tania's trip to Mérida is described in TP diary entries, January 23–26, 1952.

69. TP diary entries, January 28–29 and February 2, 1952.

70. TP diary entry, February 1, 1952.

71. TP diary entry, February 9, 1952.

72. Interview with Norma Jean Ragsdale, August 10, 2000.

73. TP diary entries, March 15–16, 1952.

74. TP diary entry, March 28, 1952.

75. TP diary entry, July 22, 1952.

76. TP diary entry, July 27, 1952.

77. TP diary entry, July 27, 1952.

78. TP diary entry, September 6, 1952.

79. TP letter to LS, September 17, 1952, UpennMA, LS file.

80. *CIW Year Book No. 52,* 294–95.

81. TP letter to Linton Satterthwaite, November 14, 1952, UpennMA, LS file.

82. *CIW Year Book No. 52,* 254.

83. TP diary entry, January 8, 1953.

84. TP diary entry, January 16, 1953.

85. *CIW Year Book No. 52,* 254, 264.

86. Tania first mentions Bernardino Euan in her diary entry of January 22, 1953. The correspondence of Bernardino Euan is from the T. Proskouriakoff Papers, 993-25, Box 1.9, PMA.

87. Telephone interview and personal correspondence from Ann Chowning, October 25, 2000.

88. The arrival of Pollock and others: TP diary entries, January 30 and February 2, 1953.

89. Telephone interview with Jerry Epstein, September 7, 2000.

90. TP diary entry, February 2, 1953.

91. Shook 1998, 93–94.

92. TP diary entries, March 9, 11, and 25, 1953.

93. TP diary entry, February 23, 1955.

94. TP diary entry, March 23, 1953.

95. Personal correspondence from Ann Chowning, October 25, 2000.

96. TP diary entry, May 12, 1953.

97. Telephone interviews with Donald E. Thompson, September 30, 1999, and Ann Chowning, November 7, 1999.

98. One colleague present at Mayapán was able to substantiate this break between Ruppert and Tania. Many people interviewed recalled Ruppert as charming and warm, though a different picture of his personality emerges in the memoirs of John O'Neill 1998, who went on an extensive expedition with Ruppert through Campeche in 1933. Details of Ruppert's career and retirement are found in *CIW Year Book No. 56*, 409, 414.

99. Perspectives on the demise of the Department of Archaeology can be found in Black 1990, 259–60; Woodbury 1973, 71–80; and Givens 1992, 112–15. The final report from the Department of Archaeology is found in the *CIW Year Book No. 57* and contains a summation of the Division's achievements.

CHAPTER NINE

1. For more on Kidder's retirement, see Woodbury 1973, 78–85; and Willey 1988, 303–14.

2. Biographical information on H. E. D. Pollock: Willey 1988, 341–42; telephone interviews with H. E. D. Pollock's son, Harry Pollock, February 10, 1999, and September 4, 2000. Also, Hill School's Alumni File and 1919 yearbook, *Dial*.

3. Willey 1988, 342–43.

4. Shook 1998, 52–58.

5. Willey 1988, 343.

6. Tania's love of Conrad is reflected throughout her diaries, as in this quote from October 30, 1955, and is confirmed in correspondence with Joyce Marcus on January 13, 1997, and in various conversations with Clemency Coggins.

7. Willey 1988, 345.

8. TP diary entry, July 26, 1940.

9. TP diary entry, January 19, 1942.

10. Week in Chichén: TP diary entries, April 18 and May 4, 1952, and Mayapán field notes, TP entry April 11, 1952, CIW Records 58-34, Box III-2#5, PMA. The depth of their personal relationship was confirmed in an interview with Gordon Willey in May 5, 1997, and corroborated in interviews with other colleagues.

11. TP diary entry, September 12, 1952.

12. TP diary entry, February 4, 1954.

13. TP diary entry, June 10, 1953.

14. TP diary entry, March 7, 1953.

15. TP diary entry, February 5, 1955.

16. Details of Strömsvik's retirement are from Olaf Husby and the letters written by Strömsvik to Tania between 1954 and 1975, Simpson Collection. The quote is from letter from Strömsvik to TP, April 5, 1957, Simpson Collection.

17. TP diary entry, July 24, 1956.

18. That Kidder persuaded the CIW to keep Tania on salary is documented in Graham 1990, 8; and confirmed in a telephone interview with Stephen Williams, September 14, 2000.

19. TP diary entry, January 1, 1954.

20. This description of Tania's apartment is from the author's personal recollections and also from a telephone interview with Richard Townsend, February 11, 1999.

21. Martha Taylor: TP diary entry June 16, 1953. Also, information from Schlesinger Library Web site.

22. Obituary notice, *Boston Globe,* March 31, 1992.

23. Cora Du Bois: "Three Generations of Anthropologists," www.peabody. harvard.edu/maria/bois.html.

24. These women friends are frequently mentioned in Tania's diary entries throughout the 1950s. Some specific references are the following: June 16, 1953; June 26, 1956; and March 24, 1958.

25. Interviews with Norma Jean Ragsdale, June 6, 1998, and January 20, 2001.

26. Letters from LS to TP, September 4, 1958, and September 7, 1954, UpennMA, LS file.

27. Interview with John Shook, December 28, 1997.

28. TP diary entry, June 18, 1957.

29. TP diary entry, March 4, 1956.

30. TP diary entry, March 8, 1956.

31. TP diary entry, March 24, 1958.

32. TP diary entry, April 9, 1958.

33. Graham 1990, 8.

34. TP diary entry, May 8, 1958.

35. Peabody appointment: TP diary entries May 24, 1958, and August 15, 1958.

36. Marcus in Gacs et al. 1988, 299.

CHAPTER TEN

1. TP diary entry, August 15, 1958.

2. TP diary entries, August 11 and 15, 1958.

3. TP diary entry, July 14, 1959.

4. Culbert 1993, 73. There are many other descriptions of Tania's breakthrough article, for example Marcus 1995, 5–7; Coe 1992, 171–76; Sabloff 1990, 89-93; Stuart in Danien and Sharer 1992, 38–40.

5. Letter from J. Eric S. Thompson to TP, May 7, 1959, Simpson Collection.

6. Letter from J. Eric S. Thompson to TP, May 16, 1962, Simpson Collection.

7. Information on Heinrich Berlin: Stuart in Danien and Sharer 1992, 38–39; and Coe 1992, 176–79.

8. TP diary entry, September 10, 1959.

9. Letter from Heinrich Berlin to TP, May 16, 1959, Simpson Collection.

10. Letter from Berlin to TP, July 27, 1959, Simpson Collection.

11. Letter from Berlin to TP, May 16, 1959, Simpson Collection.

12. Letter from LS to TP, October 8, 1957, UpennMA, LS file.

13. Letter from TP to LS, August 16, 1944, UpennMA, LS file.

14. Letter from LS to TP, March 2, 1959, UpennMA, LS file.

15. Information on David H. Kelley and Knorosov is from numerous telephone interviews with Kelley between December 7, 1998, and May 12, 1999; Stuart in Danien and Sharer 1992, 40–44; and Coe 1992, 145–66.

16. Letter from LS to TP, June 23, 1953, UpennMA, LS file.

17. TP diary entry, July 21, 1957.

18. Letter from TP to David Kelley, February 12, 1960, private papers of David H. Kelley.

19. TP diary entry, August 28, 1961.

20. Coggins biographical piece on TP in *Oxford Encyclopedia.*

21. Proskouriakoff 1961a, 14.

22. Sabloff 1990, 94.

23. Interview with David Stuart, April 9, 1998.

24. Marcus 1995, 7; personal communication with the author.

25. TP diary entry, July 2, 1959.

26. Schele and Freidel 1990, 49.

27. Marcus in Ember 1995, 7.

28. TP diary entry, September 27, 1959.

29. TP diary entry, December 4, 1959.

30. TP diary entry, December 20, 1959.

31. TP diary entry December 9, 1959.

32. TP diary entry, November 30, 1959.

33. TP diary entry, December 16, 1959, and December 20, 1959.

34. Information on Montagu came from numerous telephone interviews, including Susanna Ekholm, June 6, 2000, and Robert Laughlin, April 4, 2000. Also, personal communication with Henning Siverts (1999–2000) and conversations with Nan and Evon Vogt, October 29, 2000.

35. TP diary entry, December 20, 1959.

36. Letter from Montagu to TP, undated, Simpson Collection.

37. TP diary entry, December 10, 1959.

38. Telephone interview with Susanna Ekholm, April 10, 2000.

39. Letter from Montagu to TP, undated, Simpson Collection.

40. TP letter to Kay Beetem, February 22, 1962, PPP.

41. TP letter to Kay Beetem, March 3, 1962, PPP.

42. TP diary entry, January 15, 1962.

43. Unrest in Guatemala: TP letters to Kay, March 3, 1962, March 17, 1962, and March 19, 1962, PPP. Also, TP diary entry, March 18, 1962.

44. Shook 1998, 119–25; Coe 1999, 103–13; Harris and Ritz 1993, 327–29.

45. Letter from Robert Dyson Jr. to TP, April 29, 1962. Simpson Collection.

46. Personal correspondence from Patrick Culbert, April 22, 2000.

47. Letter from TP to Kay Beetem, April 16, 1962, PPP.

48. Information on Tania's visit to Altar de Sacrificios and Seibal is from interviews the author conducted with Gordon Willey, Jeremy Sabloff, and Ian Graham.

49. Shook 1998, 52.

50. TP diary entry, August 14, 1962.

51. Personal communication with Graham from 1972 to present; Dorfman and Slayman 1997, 50–60.

52. TP diary entry, August 22, 1966.

1. Interview with Linnea Wren, August 15, 1997, and correspondence from Wren, July 31, 1997.

2. Telephone interview with Richard Townsend, February 11, 1999. Also, Townsend entry, *Proskouriakoff Scrapbook*, n.d. Accession currently pending, PMA.

3. Letter from LS to TP, June 15, 1962, UpennMA, LS file.

4. Conference: Henning Siverts in personal correspondence, January 14, 1999. Also, Peter K. Lehnert of the Mesoamerican Heritage Institute, personal correspondence, April 20, 2000.

5. Letters from TP to Kay Beetem, April 16, 1962, and August 25, 1962, PPP.

6. Letter from TP to Kay Beetem, September 19, 1962, PPP.

7. Kornelia Kurbjuhn, personal correspondence, June 29, 2001.

8. *Worcester Art Museum News Bulletin and Calendar* 28, no. 8 (May, 1963), PPP.

9. Letter TP to Kay Beetem, May 4, 1963, PPP.

10. TP diary entry, October 2, 1962.

11. Proskouriakoff 1974b, ix–xi.

12. News Office, Harvard University Press Release, July 22, 1976. Accession File 47-52 #1b, Peabody Museum Collections Department. Also, interview with Clemency Coggins, October 29, 2000.

13. Letter from Berlin to TP, March 28, 1975, Simpson Collection.

14. Peter Lehnert, personal correspondence, May 15, 2001.

15. TP diary entry, July 14, 1970.

16. Interview with Phillippa Shaplin, July 12, 1998.

17. TP diary entry, July 15, 1970.

18. Interviews with Magdalena Ankrum, April 19, 2001, and Anastasia Korolova, June 20, 2001.

19. Galina Yershova, personal correspondence, April 27, 2001.

20. Joyce Marcus, personal correspondence, April 28, 2001.

21. TP diary entry, July 15, 1970.

22. TP diary entries, May 21 and August 2, 1963.

23. Letter from the University of Pittsburgh to TP, November 21, 1975, Simpson Collection.

24. Interview with Andrew Chenzoff, October 15, 1996.

25. Telephone interviews and personal correspondence with Joyce Marcus, 1998–2000.

26. Interviews with Gordon Willey, May 3, 1997, and October 30, 2000.

27. Proskouriakoff 1993, X.

28. Willey and Sabloff 1993, 187–88.

29. Letter from Linnea Wren, July 31, 1997. Also, telephone interview with Wren, August 15, 1997.

30. TP diary entry, April 28, 1965.

31. Interview with Jeremy Sabloff, October 30, 1997.

32. TP diary entry, May 12, 1966.

33. TP diary entry, April 14, 1966.

34. Proskouriakoff 1968d, 753.

35. Dorfman and Slayman 1997, 58–59.

36. Stuart in Danien and Sharer 1992, 45.

37. Interview with Ian Graham, May 5, 1997.

38. Letter from Graham, December 14, 2000, and interview with Coggins, October 29, 2000.

39. For more about William Spratling, see Mark 2000.

40. Letter from Spratling to TP, December 12, 1966, Simpson Collection.

41. Telephone interview with Norma Jean Ragsdale, May 20, 1997.

42. Letters from Elizabeth Benson of Dumbarton Oaks to TP, April 1, 1974, and July 22, 1976, Simpson Collection.

43. Interview with George Stuart, August 25, 1998.

44. Coe, 1992, 200.

45. Telephone interview with Elizabeth Benson, April 29, 1999.

46. Interviews with Nan Vogt, Sean Eirik Simpson, and Christopher Jones, 1997–2001.

47. Letter from Linda Schele to TP, January 17, 1977, Simpson Collection.

48. The offices of the Peabody Museum of Harvard provided the information on the Proskouriakoff Award.

49. The Pennsylvania State University Alumni Office provided information on the Woman of the Year Award.

50. Ruth Olivera, archivist of the Latin American Library of Tulane University, provided information on the ceremony.

51. Clemency Coggins kept notes and letters covering this trip with Tania and made these papers available to the author, CCC.

52. TP diary entries, January 9 and January 10, 1983.

53. Coggins 1995, 377–78.

54. Carter 1993, 102.

55. TP diary entry, January 15, 1983.

56. Easby entry, *Proskouriakoff Scrapbook*, n.d. Accession currently pending, PMA.

57. Details on the ceremony: CCC.

58. Interview with Ian Graham, May 3, 1996.

59. Typewritten message left in Tania's typewriter at the Emerson Convalescent Home, CCC.

60. Obituary, *Boston Globe*, September 11, 1985.

CHAPTER TWELVE

1. Interview with Ian Graham, May 2, 1997.

2. Interview with David Stuart, October 23, 1998, and personal correspondence from Héctor Escobedo, November 2, 1998.

3. Proskouriakoff 1963c (reprint of 1946 CIW publication), 16.

4. From a videotape of the ceremony made by Mark and Jessica Child and used with their kind permission.

5. Personal correspondence from Héctor Escobedo, November 2, 1998.

SELECTED WRITINGS OF
TATIANA PROSKOURIAKOFF

1944   "An Inscription on a Jade Probably Carved at Piedras Negras."
        *Carnegie Institution of Washington, Notes on Middle American
        Archaeology and Ethnology* 2 (47): 142–47. Washington, D.C.

1946a   *An Album of Maya Architecture.* Publication 558. Washington, D.C.:
        Carnegie Institution of Washington.

1946b   Review of *The Origins and History of the Mayas,* by M. Wells Jake-
        man. *American Anthropologist* 48: 102–5.

1950   *A Study of Classic Maya Sculpture.* Publication 593. Washington,
        D.C.: Carnegie Institution of Washington.

1951   "Some Non-Classic Traits in the Sculpture of Yucatan." In *The Civi-
        lization of Ancient America: Proceedings of the 29th International Con-
        gress of Americanists,* edited by Sol Tax, 1: 108–18. Chicago: Aldine.

1952a   "Glyphs." In S. K. Lothrop, *Metals from the Cenote of Sacrifice,
        Chichen Itza, Yucatan.* Memoirs Peabody Museum, 10 (2): 33–35.

1952b   "Sculpture and Artifacts of Mayapán." *Carnegie Institution of Wash-
        ington Year Book,* no. 51: 256–57.

1952c   "The Survival of the Maya Tun Count in Colonial Times." *Carnegie
        Institution of Washington Notes on Middle American Archaeology and
        Ethnology* 4 (112): 211–19.

1953   "Scroll Pattern (Entrelaces) of Veracruz. Huastecos, Totonacos y sus
        Vecinos." Edited by Ignacio Bernal and Eusebio Bávalos Hurtado.
        Revista Mexicana de Estudios Antropolóficos 13 (2–3): 389–401.

1954a   "Mayapán, Last Stronghold of a Civilization." *Archaeology* 7 (2):
        96–103.

1954b   "Varieties of Classic Central Veracruz Sculpture." Publication 606.
        Carnegie Institution of Washington Contribution 58: 61–94. Wash-
        ington, D.C.

1954c   Review of *The Annals of the Cakchiquels,* translated by A. Recinos
        and D. Goetz. *American Anthropologist* 56: 908.

1955a   "The Death of a Civilization." *Scientific American* 192 (5): 82–88.

1955b   Review of "Die regionale Verteilung von Schmuckelementen im
        Bereiche der Klassichen Maya-Kultur," by Wolfgang Haberland.
        American Antiquity 20 (4): 402.

1955c   With Charles R. Temple. "A Residential Quadrangle-Structures R-85 to R-90." *Carnegie Institution of Washington, Department of Archaeology, Current Reports* 1 (29): 289–361. Washington, D.C.

1956a   Reviews of "The Water Lily in Maya Art: A Complex of Alleged Aquatic Origin" and "Some Manifestations of Water in Mesoamerican Art," by Robert L. Rands. In *American Antiquity* 22 (1): 89–90.

1956b   Reviews of "Stone Monuments of the Rio Chiquito, Veracruz, Mexico," by Matthew Stirling, and "The Cerro de las Mesas Offering of Jade and Other Materials," by P. Drucker. *American Antiquity* 21 (3): 321.

1957a   Review of *The Selden Roll: An Ancient Mexican Picture Manuscript in the Bodleian Library at Oxford*, by Cottie A. Burland (commentator). *American Antiquity* 22 (3): 319.

1957b   Review of *Medieval American Art: Masterpieces of the New World before Columbus*, by Pal Kelemen. *American Antiquity* 23: 190–91.

1957c   Review of *Tombs, Temples, and Ancient Art*, by Joseph Linden Smith. *American Anthropologist* 59: 162.

1958a   Review of *Pre-Columbian Art*, by S. K. Lothrop, W. F. Foshag, and Joy Mahler. *American Antiquity* 24 (1): 201.

1958b   "Studies on Middle American Art." In *Middle American Anthropology*, edited by Gordon R. Willey, Evon Z. Vogt, and Ángel Palerm, 29–35. Pan American Union Social Science Monograph No. 5. Washington D.C.

1959   "Definitions of Maya Art and Culture." *Art Quarterly* 22: 110–26.

1960a   "Historical Implications of a Pattern of Dates at Piedras Negras, Guatemala." *American Antiquity* 25 (4): 454–75.

1960b   "Varieties of Classic Central Veracruz Sculpture." In *Contributions to American Anthropology and History* 12 (58): 61–94. Carnegie Institution of Washington, Publication 606. Washington, D.C.

1961a   "The Lords of the Maya Realm." *Expedition* 4 (1): 14–21. Reprinted in *Ancient Mesoamerica: Selected Readings*, edited by John A. Graham, 168–75. Palo Alto, Calif.: Peek, 1966.

1961b   "Portraits of Women in Maya Art." In *Essays in Pre-Columbian Art and Archaeology*, edited by Samuel K. Lothrop et al., 81–99. Cambridge, Mass.: Harvard University Press.

1962a   "Los señores del estado Maya." *Antropología e Historia de Guatemala* 14 (1): 11–17. Originally published as "The Lords of the Maya Realm," translated by Ernesto Chinchilla Aguilar.

1962b   "The Artifacts of Mayapán." In *Mayapán, Yucatán, Mexico*, edited by Harry Evelyn Dorr Pollock et al., 321–442. Carnegie Institution of Washington, Publication 619. Washington, D.C.

1962c   "Civic and Religious Structures of Mayapan." In *Mayapán, Yucatán, México*, edited by Harry Evelyn Dorr Pollock et al., 87–164. Carnegie Institution of Washington, Publication 619. Washington, D.C.

1962d   Review of *More Human than Divine: An Intimate and Lively Self-Portrait in Clay of a Smiling People from Ancient Veracruz*, by William Spratling, *American Antiquity* 27 (4): 439.

1962e   Review of "Tikal Reports Numbers 5–10," by Richard E. W. Adams, Vivian L. Broman, William R. Coe, William A. Haviland Jr., Ruben E. Reina, Linton Satterthwaite, Edwin M. Shook, and Aubrey S. Trik. *American Antiquity* 28: 117.

1963a   "Historical Data in the Inscriptions of Yaxchilan, Part I." *Estudios de Cultura Maya* 3: 149–67. Mexico City: Universidad Nacional Autónomo de México.

1963b   Review of *The Art and Architecture of Ancient America: The Mexican, Maya, and Andean Peoples*, by George Kubler. *American Journal of Archaeology* 67 (3): 323–24.

1963c   Reprint of *An Album of Maya Architecture*. Norman: University of Oklahoma Press.

1964a   "El arte Maya y el modelo genético de cultura." In *Desarrollo cultural de los Mayas*, edited by Evon Z. Vogt and Alberto Ruz Lhuillier, 179–93. Mexico: Universidad Nacional Autónomo de Mexico.

1964b   "Historical Data in the Inscriptions of Yaxchilan, Part II." *Estudios de Cultura Maya* 4: 177–201. Mexico City: Universidad Nacional Autónoma de Mexico.

1965a   "Sculpture and Major Arts of the Maya Lowlands." In *Handbook of Middle American Indians*, vol. 2, edited by Gordon R. Willey, 469–97. Austin: University of Texas Press.

1965b   Review of *Maya Jades*, by Adrian Digby. *American Antiquity* 30: 360–61.

1966   Review of "An Early Stone Pectoral from Southeastern Mexico," by Michael Coe. *American Antiquity* 31 (6): 887–89.

1968a   "Olmec and Maya Art: Problems of Their Stylistic Relation." In *Dumbarton Oaks Conference on the Olmec*, edited by Elizabeth P. Benson, 119–34. Washington, D.C.: Dumbarton Oaks.

1968b   "The Jog and Jaguar Signs in Maya Writing." *American Antiquity* 33 (2): 247–51.

1968c   *Graphic Designs on Mesoamerican Pottery*. Washington, D.C.: Carnegie Institution of Washington.

1968d   "Suzanna Whitelaw Miles, 1922–1966." *American Anthropologist* 70: 753–54.

1969   *Álbum de arquitectura Maya*. Mexico City: Fondo de Cultura Económico.

1970a   "On Two Inscriptions from Chichen Itza." *Papers of the Peabody Museum of Archaeology and Ethnology* 61: 457–67. Cambridge, Mass.: Harvard University.

1970b   Review of *Studies in Classic Maya Iconography*, by George Kubler. *American Journal of Archaeology* 74: 315–16.

1971a   "Classic Art of Central Veracruz." In *Handbook of Middle American Indians*, vol. 11, edited by Gordon F. Ekholm and Ignacio Bernal, 558–72. Austin: University of Texas Press.

1971b   "Early Architecture and Sculpture in Mesoamerica." *University of California Archaeological Research Facility, Contribution* 11, 141–56. Berkeley: University of California Press.

1972   Review of *Kultura Drevnikh Maya*, by R. Kinzhalov. *American Anthropologist* 74: 36–37.

1973   "The Hand-Grasping-Fish and Associated Glyphs on Classic Maya Monuments." In *Mesoamerican Writing Systems: A Conference at Dumbarton Oaks*, edited by Elizabeth P. Benson, 165–78. Washington, D.C.: Dumbarton Oaks.

1974a   "Calendar Systems of the Americas." In *Encyclopedia Britannica*, 15th ed., 609–12.

1974b   *Jades from the Cenote of Sacrifice, Chichen Itza*. Memoirs of the Peabody Museum, Harvard University, vol. 10, no. 1. Cambridge, Mass.

1978a   "Maya Jade Plaque; Maya Jade Head." In *Masterpieces of the Peabody Museum*, 62, 63. Cambridge, Mass.: Peabody Museum, Harvard University.

1978b   "Olmec Gods and Maya God-Glyphs." *Human Mosaic* 12: 113–17.

1980   "Maize-God: The Symbol of *Symbols*." *Symbols* (Summer): 8–10.

1984   "Incidents of Ancient Maya History." *Proceedings of the American Philosophical Society* 128 (2): 164–66.

1993   *Maya History*. Austin: University of Texas Press.

BIBLIOGRAPHY

Baedeker, Karl. 1912. *Norway, Sweden, and Denmark*. New York: Scribner's.

Berg, A. Scott. 1998. *Lindberg*. New York: G. P. Putnam's Sons.

Bezilla, Michael. 1985. *Penn State: An Illustrated History*. University Park: Pennsylvania State University Press.

Bishop, Ronald L., and Frederick W. Lange, ed. 1991. *The Ceramic Legacy of Anna O. Shepard*. Niwot: University Press of Colorado.

Black, Stephen L. 1990. "The Carnegie Uaxactún Project and the Development of Maya Archaeology." *Ancient Mesoamerica* 1: 256–76.

Blaser, Werner. 1994. *Tomsk: Texture in Wood*. Berlin: Birkhauser.

Bourne, Edward W., ed. 1919. *The History of the Class of Nineteen Hundred and Nineteen—Yale*. New Haven: Yale University Press.

Brenner, Anita, and George R. Leighton. [1943] 1971. *The Wind That Swept Mexico*. Reprint. Austin: University of Texas Press.

Brigham, William T. [1887] 1965. *Guatemala, the Land of the Quetzal*. Reprint, with an introduction by Wilson Popenoe. Gainesville: University of Florida Press.

Brunhouse, Robert L. 1971. *Sylvanus G. Morley and the World of the Ancient Mayas*. Norman: University of Oklahoma Press.

———. 1973. *In Search of the Maya*. Albuquerque: University of New Mexico Press.

———. 1975. *Pursuit of the Ancient Maya*. Albuquerque: University of New Mexico Press.

———. 1976. *Frans Blom, Maya Explorer*. Albuquerque: University of New Mexico Press.

Buck, Pearl S. 1941. *Of Men and Women*. New York: John Day.

Buckley, Tom. 1984. *Violent Neighbors: El Salvador, Central America, and the United States*. New York: Times Books.

Burns, E. Bradford. 1994. *Latin America, a Concise Interpretive History*. Englewood Cliffs, N.J.: Prentice Hall.

Canning, Fairfax. 1923. *Siberia's Untouched Treasure*. New York: Knickerbocker Press.

Carnegie, Andrew. 1920. *Autobiography of Andrew Carnegie*. Boston: Houghton Mifflin Company.

Carnegie Institution of Washington. 1942–58. *Year Book*. Nos. 42–58. Washington, D.C.: Carnegie Institution of Washington.

Carter, Edward C., II, 1993. *"One Grand Pursuit": A Brief History of the American Philosophical Society's First 250 Years, 1743–1993*. Philadelphia: American Philosophical Society.

Chadha, Yogesh. 1997. *Gandhi, a Life*. New York: John Wiley.

Chandler, Alfred D., and Stephen Salsbury. 1971. *Pierre S. Du Pont and the Making of the Modern Corporation*. New York: Harper and Row.

Cipriani, Christine, ed. 1998. *Fodor's Belize and Guatemala*. New York: Fodor's Travel Publications.

Claassen, Cheryl, ed. 1994. *Women in Archaeology*. Philadelphia: University of Pennsylvania Press.

Coe, Michael D. 1992. *Breaking the Maya Code*. London: Thames and Hudson.

———. 1993. *The Maya*. 5th ed. London: Thames and Hudson.

———. 1999. *The Maya*. 6th ed. London: Thames and Hudson.

Coggins, Clemency. 1995. Review of *Maya History*, by Tatiana Proskouriakoff, edited by R. A. Joyce. *Latin American Antiquity* 6 (4): 377–78.

Coggins, Clemency, and Orrin Shane. 1984. *Cenote of Sacrifice*. Austin: University of Texas Press.

Connell, Evan S., Jr., 1974. *The Connoisseur*. New York: Alfred A. Knopf.

Culbert, T. Patrick. 1993. *Maya Civilization*. Montreal and Washington, D.C.: St. Remy Press and Smithsonian Institution Press.

Danien, Elin, and Robert J. Sharer, eds. 1992. *New Theories on the Ancient Maya*. University Museum Monograph 77. Philadelphia: University Museum, University of Pennsylvania.

Dorfman, John, and Andrew L. Slayman. 1997. "Maverick Mayanist." *Archaeology* 50 (5): 50–60.

Dukes, Paul. 1974. *A History of Russia: Medieval, Modern and Contemporary*. New York: McGraw-Hill.

Evans, Harold. 1998. *The American Century*. New York: Alfred A. Knopf.

Fadiman, Clifton, ed. 1939. *I Believe: The Personal Philosophies of Certain Eminent Men and Women of Our Time*. New York: Simon and Schuster.

Fagan, Brian M. 1991. *Kingdoms of Gold, Kingdoms of Jade*. London: Thames and Hudson.

Fash, William L. 1991. *Scribes, Warriors and Kings: The City of Copan and the Ancient Maya*. London: Thames and Hudson.

Foster, Lynn V. 1997. *A Brief History of Mexico*. New York: Facts on File.

Gacs, Ute, Aisha Khan, Jerrie McIntyre, and Ruth Weinberg, eds. 1988. *Women Anthropologists: A Biographical Dictionary*. New York: Greenwood Press.

Gilbert, Martin. 1994. *The First World War: A Complete History*. New York: Henry Holt.

Givens, Douglas R. 1992. *Alfred Vincent Kidder and the Development of Americanist Archaeology*. Albuquerque: University of New Mexico Press.

Graham, Ian. 1990. "Tatiana Proskouriakoff (1909–1985)." *American Antiquity* 55 (1): 6–11.

Halle, Louis, Jr. 1941. *River of Ruins*. New York: Henry Holt.

Hare, Richard. 1947. *Russian Literature from Pushkin to the Present Day*. Freeport, N.Y.: Books for Libraries Press.

Harris, Richard, and Stacy Ritz. 1993. *The Maya Route: The Ultimate Guidebook*. Berkeley, Calif.: Ulysses Press.

Hatch, Alden. 1956. *Remington Arms in American History*. New York: Rinehart.

Hay, Clarence L., et al. [1940] 1977. *The Maya and Their Neighbors: Essays on Middle American Anthropology and Archaeology*. New York: Dover Publications.

Herring, Hubert. 1972. *A History of Latin America from the Beginnings to the Present*. New York: Alfred A. Knopf.

Houston, Stephen D., Oswaldo Chinchilla Mazriegos, and David Stuart, eds. 2001. *The Decipherment of Ancient Maya Writing*. Norman: University of Oklahoma Press.

Howard, Michael, and W. Roger Louis, eds. 1998. *The Oxford History of the Twentieth Century*. New York: Oxford University Press.

Hughes, Lindsey. 1998. *Russia in the Age of Peter the Great*. New Haven: Yale University Press.

Ignatieff, Michael. 1987. *The Russian Album*. New York: Viking.

Knorozov, Yuri V., with Tatiana Proskouriakoff. 1967. *The Writing of the Maya Indians*. Translated by Sophie Coe. Russian Translation series, vol. 4. Cambridge, Mass.: Peabody Museum of Archaeology and Ethnology.

Kochan, Miriam. 1976. *The Last Days of Imperial Russia*. New York: Macmillan.

Krauze, Enrique. 1997. *Mexico: Biography of Power*. New York: HarperCollins.

Kropotkin, P. 1905. *Russian Literature*. New York: Benjamin Blom.

Lincoln, W. Bruce. 1994. *The Conquest of a Continent: Siberia and the Russians*. New York: Random House.

Lothrop, Eleanor. 1948. *Throw Me a Bone: What Happens When You Marry an Archaeologist*. New York: Whittlesey House; McGraw-Hill.

Lothrop, Samuel K., W. C. Root, and Tatiana Proskouriakoff. 1952. *Metals from the Cenote of Sacrifice, Chichén Itzá, Yucatán*. Memoirs of the Peabody Museum of Archaeology and Ethnology 10 (2). Cambridge: Harvard University Press.

Lothrop, Samuel K., et al. 1961. *Essays in Pre-Columbian Art and Archaeology.* Cambridge, Mass.: Harvard University Press.

Madeira, Percy C. 1964. *Men in Search of Man.* Philadelphia: University of Pennsylvania Press.

Mallan, Chicki. 1994. *Central Mexico Handbook.* Chico, Calif.: Moon Publications.

Marcus, Joyce. 1976. *Emblem and State in the Classic Maya Lowlands.* Washington, D.C.: Dumbarton Oaks.

———. 1995. "Maya Hieroglyphs: History or Propaganda?" In *Research Frontiers in Anthropology,* edited by Carol Ember and Mel Ember 1–24. Englewood Cliffs, N.J.: Prentice-Hall.

Mark, Joan. 2000. *The Silver Gringo: William Spratling and Taxco.* Albuquerque: University of New Mexico Press.

Mead, Margaret. 1972. *Blackberry Winter.* New York: William Morrow.

Mercer, Henry. 1975. *The Hill-Caves of Yucatan,* with a new introduction by Sir J. Eric S. Thompson. Norman: University of Oklahoma Press.

Miller, Mary Ellen. 1995. "Maya Masterpiece Revealed at Bonampak." *National Geographic* 187 (2): 50–69.

———. 1999. *Maya Art and Architecture.* London: Thames and Hudson.

Morley, Sylvanus G. 1920. *The Inscriptions at Copan.* Publication 219. Washington, D.C.: Carnegie Institution of Washington.

———. 1938. *The Inscriptions of Peten.* 5 vols. Publication 437. Washington, D.C.: Carnegie Institution of Washington.

———. 1946. *The Ancient Maya.* Stanford: Stanford University Press.

Morris, Elizabeth Ann. 1974. "Anna O. Shepard, 1903–1973." *American Antiquity* 39 (3): 448–51.

Moynahan, Brian. 1994. *The Russian Century.* New York: Random House.

O'Neill, John P. 1998. *Yucatan Alternative.* Chapel Hill: Duke–UNC Program of Latin American Studies.

Parezo, Nancy J., ed. 1993. *Hidden Scholars: Women Anthropologists and the Native American Southwest.* Albuquerque: University of New Mexico Press.

Pohl, John M. D. 1999. *Exploring Mesoamerica.* New York: Oxford University Press.

Pollock, H. E. D. 1980. *The Puuc.* Cambridge, Mass.: Peabody Museum, Harvard University.

Pollock, H. E. D., Ralph L. Roys, T. Proskouriakoff, and A. Ledyard Smith. 1962. *Mayapan, Yucatan, Mexico.* Publication 619. Washington, D.C.: Carnegie Institution of Washington.

Rayfield, Donald. 1997. *Anton Chekhov, a Life*. New York: Henry Holt.

Reyman, Jonathan, ed. 1992. *Rediscovering Our Past: Essays on the History of American Archaeology*. Brookfield, Vt.: Avebury Press.

Riasanovsky, Nicholas V. 1977. *A History of Russia*. 3rd ed. New York: Oxford University Press.

Robicsek, Francis. 1972. *Copan: Home of the Mayan Gods*. New York: Museum of the American Indian, Heye Foundation.

Ruppert, Karl, and John H. Denison, Jr. 1943. *Archaeological Reconnaissance in Campeche, Quintana Roo, and Peten*. Publication 543. Washington, D.C.: Carnegie Institution of Washington.

Ruppert, Karl, J. Eric S. Thompson, and Tatiana Proskouriakoff. 1955. *Bonampak, Chiapas, Mexico*. Publication 602. Washington, D.C.: Carnegie Institution of Washington.

Sabloff, Jeremy. 1990. *The New Archaeology and the Ancient Maya*. New York: Scientific American Library.

Satterthwaite, Linton. 1943. *Piedras Negras Archaeology*. Philadelphia: University Museum, University of Pennsylvania.

Schele, Linda, and David Freidel. 1990. *A Forest of Kings*. New York: William Morrow.

Schultz, Matthew. 1996. *Views of Lansdowne*. Dover, N.H.: Arcadia Publishing.

Sharer, Robert. 1994. *The Ancient Maya*. 5th ed. Stanford: Stanford University Press.

Shenk, Hiram H. 1932. *Encyclopedia of Pennsylvania*. Harrisburg: National Historical Association.

Shook, Edwin M. 1990. "Recollections of a Maya Archaeologist." *Ancient Mesoamerica* 1 (2): 247–52.

———. 1998. *Incidents in the Life of a Maya Archaeologist as Told to Winifred Veronda*. Guatemala City: Southwestern Academy Press.

Shook, Edwin M., and Elayne Marquis. 1996. *Secrets in Stone Yokes, Hachas and Palmas from Southern Mesoamerica*. Philadelphia: American Philosophical Society.

Shook, Edwin M. and Tatiana Proskouriakoff. 1956. "Settlement Patterns in Mesoamerica and the Sequence in the Guatemalan Highlands." In *Prehistoric Settlement Patterns in the New World*, edited by Gordon R. Willey, 93–100. Publications in Anthropology, no. 23. New York: Wenner-Gren Foundation for Anthropological Research.

Smith, A. Ledyard. 1955. *Archaeological Reconnaissance in Central Guatemala*. Publication 608. Washington, D.C.: Carnegie Institution of Washington.

————. 1982. *Excavations at Seibal, Department of Peten, Guatemala: Major Architecture and Caches*. Memoirs, vol. 15, no. 1. Cambridge, Mass.: Peabody Museum, Harvard University.

Smith, Michael E. 1996. *The Aztecs*. Cambridge, Mass.: Blackwell.

Stuart, David. 1999. "The Maya Finally Speak." *Discovering Archaeology* (November–December). www.discoveringarchaeology.com/0699toc/6cover 8-maya.shtml.

Stuart, George E. 1989. "Copan: City of Kings and Commoners." *National Geographic Magazine* 176, (4): 488–504.

Stuart, George E., and Gene S. Stuart. 1977. *The Mysterious Maya*. Washington, D.C.: National Geographic Society.

Tayler, Jeffrey. 1999. *Siberian Dawn: A Journey across the New Russia*. St. Paul, Minn.: Hungry Mind Press.

Taylor, A. J. P., ed. 1974. *History of World War I*. London: Octopus Books.

Thompson, John Eric Sidney. 1963. *Maya Archaeologist*. Norman: University of Oklahoma Press.

Thompson, J. Eric S., and T. Proskouriakoff. 1947. "Maya Calendar Round Dates Such as 9 Ahau 17 Mol." *Carnegie Institution of Washington, Division of Historical Research. Notes on Middle American Archaeology and Ethnology* 3 (79): 143–50.

Wauchope, Robert. 1965. *They Found the Buried Cities*. Chicago: University of Chicago Press.

Wall, Joseph Frazier. 1970. *Andrew Carnegie*. New York: Oxford University Press.

Weinberg, Gerhard L. 1994. *A World at Arms: A Global History of World War II*. Cambridge: Cambridge University Press.

Wendt, Herbert. 1966. *The Red, White, and Black Continent: Latin America, Land of Reformers and Rebels*. Garden City, N.Y.: Doubleday.

Whipperman, Bruce. 1995. *Pacific Mexico Handbook*. Chico, Calif.: Moon Publications.

Willey, Gordon R. 1987. *Essays in Maya Archaeology*. Albuquerque: University of New Mexico Press.

————. 1988. *Portraits in American Archaeology*. Albuquerque: University of New Mexico Press.

Willey, Gordon R., and Jeremy Sabloff. 1993. *A History of American Archaeology*. 3rd ed. New York: W. H. Freeman.

Williams, Adriana. 1994. *Covarrubias*. Austin: University of Texas Press.

Williamson, Harold F. 1952. *Winchester, the Gun That Won the West*. Washington, D.C.: Combat Forces Press.

Woodbury, Richard B. 1973. *Alfred V. Kidder*. New York: Columbia University Press.

Woodward, Ralph Lee, Jr. 1976. *Central America, a Nation Divided*. New York: Oxford University Press.

Yagoda, Ben. 1993. *Will Rogers, a Biography*. New York: Alfred A. Knopf.

Zimmer, Heinrich. 1951. *Philosophies of India*. New York: Bollingen Foundation.

INDEX